GRIEF RECOVERY WORKBOOK

Fitzgerald

GRIEF RECOVERY WORKBOOK

Helping You Weather the Storms of Death, Divorce, and Overwhelming Disappointments

"CHAPLAIN RAY" GIUNTA

with Cathy Giunta

INTEGRITY®
PUBLISHERS
Nashville

I would like to dedicate this book to all of those who have suffered a loss, journeyed the road of grief, and found the love in their hearts to share their experiences. Without your strength, courage, and commitment to help others, this guide for people who are just beginning their journeys would not have been possible.

Contents

Foreword

The following workbook has been designed as a step-by-step self-help course for those experiencing catastrophic loss of any kind. It can also be used as curriculum by individuals in a group setting, and is a training tool for those wanting to become compassionate care providers. I have trained thousands of people who have wanted to know what to say, what to do, how to help in the everyday crises of life as well as in national crises.

Anyone, everyone, can be a "chaplain" on some level to the survivors of crises in his or her spheres of influence. There are tragedies every day happening all around us. In fact, that is how I first began this work. In 1987, I had seen the newspaper headline reporting the tragic deaths of two small boys who were hit by a car while riding a tricycle. It had caught my eye and my heart. I suddenly wondered who was helping their single mothers with the practical matters of the tragedy. Who was helping them pick up the pieces, bury the boys properly, cope with the arrangements and the costs? I found out the answer—no one was helping them. No social services group can meet all the needs of the traumatized. They were about to fall through the cracks of society's official safety nets. So I volunteered. We Care, our organization providing compassionate crisis care, was begun that simply. Our compassionate Christian social work began slowly to fill a growing gap in crisis care, and the work ultimately included the nation's escalating number of mass tragedies, from school shootings to terrorists bombings, including sixty-eight days at Ground Zero after the World Trade Center attack on September 11, 2001.

If you are interested in using this workbook as a self-training tool, I commend you and direct you to the back to Appendix 2, which is an addition to the workbook course provided just for you. You'll also notice that a CD has been included in this volume. It contains prayerful, chapter-by-chapter guidance for moving beyond your loss and reaching out to others. Finally, feel free to contact us for our audio series, which captures the material as it was taught in a live setting to people who came for healing and training. Twelve audio tape sessions are available to assist you as you go through this book.

Now begin the workbook, choosing a loss from your own life to examine as you go. And please contact us at any time at *www.wecare4u.org*.

Serving you,
Chaplain Ray and Cathy Giunta

Take Only Memories,
Leave Only Footprints

Each day, I take my morning walk. Down the steep hill I go, over the concrete bridge that covers the seasonal creek and then turning right at the end of the bridge. By this point, I am deep in my thoughts of praise and adoration for God as I enter a nearby wilderness preserve through the rear gate.

Traveling a path covered by a canopy of black oaks and lined with berry bushes, I come to the entrance of the nature center near the preserve's front gate. I have walked this way on many days sharing my fears, failures, and hopes with the One who loves all of us. On one fog-filled winter day, though, I noticed something different. There, to my right, almost hidden by the undergrowth, was a sign with this message: "Take only memories, leave only footprints." The weathered old sign had probably stood as a sentry, greeting the wilderness visitors for years, reminding folks like me to tread lightly in this beautiful place. On that morning, though, it would also suggest something different to me.

I hadn't taken this morning walk in a few days; I had been gone, working with survivors of a tragedy in another city. I had them on my mind when I saw the motto, and a thought occurred to me: *Those inscribed words also could be applied to another kind of wilderness we all face in life—the wilderness experience of loss.* Perhaps the Creator of both nature and humanity means for us to approach our grief recovery just that way: Take only memories. Leave only footprints.

We always leave something of ourselves after a loss, don't we? Some leave their joy, never believing they'll laugh again. Others vow to leave their heart with the person who has forever gone. Still others leave their desire to live. And some, when they can no longer take the pain, leave their very lives. And whatever we take is rarely what is going to help us through our crisis.

Regardless of the type of loss you have experienced—be it death, divorce, separation, illness, professional setbacks, betrayal of trust or friendship—any loss produces grief. Any loss is some form of death, an ending which changes everything, and we deal with loss in many ways, using healthy and unhealthy means to process it. Some people simply medicate themselves, hoping to survive the pain until it goes away. Others attempt to ignore it—working harder, praying longer, and doing more worthy deeds. Others, overwhelmed with the flood of aching emotions, find self-destructive answers—alcohol, prescribed and illicit drugs, unhealthy attachments, or even promiscuity. These solutions only provide temporary relief, though, not a clear path through grief. I have counseled thousands of people through this journey—in living rooms and at national disaster sites—and have seen all kinds of resolutions to loss. And far too often, I see people defeated by the loss, losing their way, never moving into life again.

But that's not you.

You have picked up this workbook because you have had a loss thrust upon you, and now you want to help yourself handle it. You may be feeling a flood of things or nothing at all, but I have no doubt that you feel you have been left at the entrance to your own personal wilderness—and you are lost. And yet here is the good news: You are already looking for signposts to help you find your way through grief's wilderness.

Let me direct you to another one. On this wintry morning, let's take a few more steps into my wilderness preserve to another sign that seems also to be custom-made for us. A few steps farther, the path divides and the trailhead sign shows two directional arrows offering two types of walks.

The left arrow is inscribed: *Observation.*

The right arrow is inscribed: *Discovery.*

That applies to your grief process as well. If you have no desire for direction, follow the Observation path. You won't see any more markers, just areas that allow passive observation of anything that happens along the way. Anything hidden in the forest will be missed.

But if you choose the Discovery path, you may learn about what you see—and what you don't see. Signs are posted along the way to teach you as you follow the wilderness path.

Picking up this workbook is like taking the Discovery path through the wilderness of grief you find yourself in. You are going to take an inward journey. For some the discovery is just to find their way through the forest. Others may find deep meaning in the journey, as well as things about themselves and others which they'd never seen before. Still others will end the journey strong enough to leave signposts of their own for others to discover.

You don't have to be a survival expert to journey through your loss. You just have to be brave enough to start the journey—and smart enough to choose the path of discovery. The goal of grief recovery is not to take away all pain. This side of eternity, that remains impossible. The workbook you hold, though, is a walk through your grief experience that can teach as well as comfort and guide. In the pages that follow, you can find what you need to safely make the journey.

Let's take it together. And I pray that our journey will end with your discovery that you have taken only memories and have left only footprints on your way "home."

> ## For additional encouragement, listen to Number 1 on the *Grief Recovery Workbook CD*

Chapter 1

Your Loss Is Not Fair

A good friend of ours died of cancer recently. For nine years, she battled it. Her daughter had been four years old when she was diagnosed. The mother set herself a goal—to see her daughter graduate high school. She lived only to see her daughter finish sixth grade...

A woman who has struggled to have a child for six years finally becomes a mother. One day when she goes in to check on her newborn, she finds the baby dead—a victim of Sudden Infant Death Syndrome...

After devoting her life to supporting her workaholic husband, a woman is left alone when her husband leaves her to marry someone else...

A man survives eight days under a collapsed bridge after the San Francisco earthquake, only to die in the hospital after being rescued...

A New York City family creates and posts hundreds of "missing person" posters when their father doesn't come home from work on September 11, 2001, at the World Trade Center...

A husband faithfully supports and cheers on his wife as she overcomes a debilitating illness, then becomes terminally ill himself...

"It's not fair!"

I have heard these words uttered, sometimes screamed, a thousand times as I have worked with those being forced to face a devastating loss. The pain they describe could melt granite.

I remember one of the first times those words hit home. My wife, four months pregnant with our first child, was suddenly visiting the hospital almost every day, but not just for prenatal checkup and care. Her father was dying. He was a good man who loved God, his family, and his country. He served a career in the U.S. Army working in the hospital units. After retiring from the military, he became a postman. He was also an expert at clock repair. He loved big clocks, like the large, German grandfather clock that majestically echoed its song throughout the entire house. On a sleepless night it would be an ever-constant reminder of the faithfulness of God.

> And being in anguish, [Jesus] prayed more earnestly.
>
> *Luke 22:44*

A year earlier, he'd felt ill, but after tests the doctor sent him home with the assurance that all was well and he would soon feel better again. Months went by, but as his second retirement approached—the one that would allow him all the time in the world for his clocks and his loved ones—he began once again to feel poorly.

This time, though, his doctor had a different prognosis. Apparently there was a mistake and, indeed, Raymond wasn't well and hadn't been for some time. After more tests, the diagnosis was clear; he had cancer. Only months before his first grandchild was born, he died.

It was just not fair.

Loss always takes us by surprise; it's never an invited guest. We never wake up one day and say, "I am sure planning for a big loss today." If that were the case, you would pull the covers over your head, close the blinds, bolt the doors, and not even get out of bed.

We approach every day with a positive new sense of something special and good happening, don't we? "Today I will get that job, buy that car, get married, or have a baby. Today my child will get an A on her spelling test; I'll complete my work project." Each day of life starts as a new adventure. And then it happens. When we least expect it, loss barges in. Life has just changed, probably forever, and we are so unprepared. And the grief process begins.

The truth is, grief is a part of being human, and we are 100 percent human. And at the heart of *that* truth is the obvious fact that God made us to experience it. We are not protected from earthly sorrows. Bad things are going to happen to God's people. However good it sounds, whatever anyone has told or promised you, being a person of faith does not free us from heartache.

Perspective is everything when we experience loss. Some people deal with loss fatalistically. They just throw up their hands when something awful happens to them: "We can't do anything about loss, so why try?" Others are expecting something awful to always be looming in the shadows, knowing that disappointment and pain are inevitable. Each day offers another chance that grief will strike. They are gripped with fear and no longer really live any kind of quality daily existence. And others resort to saying all sorts of heroic things to get through the trauma and back to some semblance of a normal life. "Stay strong." "Just fight through it." "Pick yourself up by your bootstraps."

I agree with some of these perspectives. Loss *is* certain. For some, the losses will be numerous. For others, they'll be lucky enough to count their life's losses on one hand. I don't agree that we are powerless. We can do something about loss, and we should do something about loss. Part of the problem today is that we don't deal well with our losses. The pain is so bad, we see nothing clearly; in fact we often grope blindly for someone or something to blame. And the blame seems to fall into three categories. Do these sound familiar?

1. *If God is a loving God, why did this happen?*
2. *How could I have let this happen?*
3. *I will never be able to forgive (insert name)_____. It is all his/her fault.*

To begin a journey of any kind, the first thing any traveler needs is to see clearly. I think you'll agree that any journey begun with any of those three perspectives has little chance of ending well. You can almost see how rough those chosen roads are going to be.

In the past fifteen years of working as a crisis chaplain and training and teaching others to cope with the fallout of loss, I've formulated another way to confront this inevitable part of life: We can change our view.

A NEW PAIR OF GLASSES

Eyeglasses are an amazing invention. Glass is shaped to make up for noted deficiencies in the eyes. When the proper lens is placed in front of the near- or farsighted eye, the view changes—the blurry becomes transparent, the vision crystal clear. A new pair of glasses gives a brand new perspective on everything in sight.

Let's craft a new lens to assist you with your grief process.

DEATH OF A DREAM

Recently, I met an eighteen-year-old who doesn't dream anymore.

"What do you want to do?" I casually asked him.

I don't want to do anything," he answered.

"No, I mean, what do you want to do with your life? Do you want to be a teacher, a policeman, fireman or what?"

He said, "No, really, I don't want to do anything." We talked for an hour. And he finally admitted that he had failed in something very important to him two years earlier and ever since then he'd had no ambition to do anything anymore. He was stuck, chronically grieving a death of a dream.

Any loss is a death of some kind, even if it isn't a literal end of life. Every loss is a death of something, be it a loved one, a relationship, a sense of security, even a dream. The loss of a job can bring about the process of grief. A dream of one's future has died.

SELF-CHECK

Circle any (or all) of the grief perspectives below you have felt recently:

• Blaming others   • Blaming yourself   • Blaming God

Even retirement can create grief. It's not strange to hear about people who have died shortly after retiring. Grief can set in with the death of a way of life and can be deadly itself if not dealt with.

The death of a dream could be a physical loss or immobility. A mother of a disabled child once told me she has grieved over the loss of her child's health and the dream she had for his future. The death could be the loss of finances—perhaps bankruptcy and the fear that creates. It could be the loss of your character or your credibility, or the death of a marriage—the broken trust of divorce or unfaithfulness. And we all know how one death can cause another, when the resulting grief isn't handled well by the survivors. All too often we hear, after an elderly person's death, of the spouse dying quickly thereafter.

Whatever the origin of your loss, it is a death of some kind. And all death leaves grief in its wake. As the days go by, sometimes that personal loss is the only perspective you can muster.

SELF-CHECK

- What is your loss? Is it the death of a dream? How would you express it?

_____

_____

_____

_____

_____

_____

_____

A GOD'S-EYE VIEW

"It's not fair."

Our sense of justice comes from somewhere, and it has to be part of being made in God's image. Animals don't have a concept of fairness, and yet most of us humans innately demand fairness. In fact, we are famous as a nation for it—the American sense of fair play. Even though we rarely see it in life, we expect it. So we demand from God an accounting, a fairness regarding what happens to us here on earth.

While we may or may not believe in a real Satan who is controlling the evil on this earth, our first response always seems to blame God. After all, he is in control, isn't he? Yes and no— we know this from our Christian theology. We know that God has allowed us to have the freedom to enjoy the world and the choice whether to have a relationship with him. And we know that our freedom's dark side has changed everything. And we know, in an unheralded gesture that changed everything yet again, God reached out to us by coming in human form.

So, like awareness itself, the sense of fairness must come from the One who created us. It makes no sense otherwise. And that is the perspective most of us need in order to feel a sense of fairness in life: We need God's perspective. We need a way to see beyond our heart's hurt to what our head is telling us is true—to see God's big picture. That perspective is an acquired thing, though. It's like a pair of new glasses that enable us to read our recovery road's signposts and find our way to a productive and mature future.

> I cried out to God for help; I cried out to God to hear me.
>
> *Psalm 77:1*

In the pages ahead, you won't find any response to the unfairness of your loss. There isn't one. But there are other answers for the grief process you're now forced to handle. Those answers come from years of my own professional discovery—listening to, watching, and learning from people like you. As I've worked with grieving people in all kinds of crises—the kind that make newspaper headlines and the kind that only imprint their headlines on grieving hearts—I've applied what I know from God's biblical resource. Together we can see what the truth has to say in the context of your loss, because it's that truth that sets us free. We all will have loss; but everyone has the option of seeing it through God's eyes, and that can be a great comfort.

Gaining a new perspective about your loss has to be a choice, but it's not an easy one, nor is it one that you may be able to choose wholly at this moment. You may need more information, more thought, more time to discover. You may even need to acknowledge your resistance to a God's-eye-view perspective if you are struggling with how you see God's role in your loss. You may be angry at God. And worse, you may feel you have to stifle that anger of all angers. But it's just not so. In fact, anger is one of the many pivotal issues worthy of more time, more information, more thought.

> "You will weep and mourn while the world rejoices.
> You will grieve, but your grief will turn to joy."
>
> *John 16:20*

That's why I've fashioned this workbook to be a progressive, step-by-step discovery experience. Little by little, page by page, you will be allowing yourself time to process only the amount of information, thought, and discovery you need for that day. Each page will share what I've learned in fourteen years of working with crisis and our human response to it—both healthy and unhealthy. Each page will offer you a progressively new perspective with which to view what is happening to you.

Your life has already changed with your loss. But the good news is this: Your life can change again—at your own speed, through your own work, in the spaces ahead.

So let's begin.

Work It Out

Sometimes you need a new perspective to help your head see through the pain of your hurting heart. Consider the questions below:

1. Think about the loss you have experienced. If you listen to your heart, why did it happen and who is to blame?

_____

_____

_____

_____

2. What do you think your head might be telling you about your perspective that your grieving heart might not be able to hear?

_____

_____

_____

_____

3. How do you think God is seeing you in your loss?

_____

_____

_____

_____

4. How do you see God right now? Do you see God as "raising his hand" against you? Or are you seeing him as a loving Father with arms open wide, wanting to heal your hurt?

_____

_____

_____

_____

To Journal Is to Heal

At the end of each chapter of your workbook you will find journal space for recording your thoughts. This may be the biggest favor you do yourself.

Take a moment. Give yourself a chance to process, to consider, to switch your mental gears from the emotions of grief you are *feeling* into words you are *thinking* about your grief and your discoveries. Your journal is private—it's a safe place to say what you really feel. Then later you can look back and see how you're changing and growing.

Write about what is happening to you as you face this recovery process—what you are learning—and watch what happens. There's real power and catharsis in seeing on paper how you feel.

Make your entry a letter to someone. Feel free to change to whom you are writing as you move along. Today it may be a trusted friend; tomorrow, God; the next day, consider writing to me; and the next day to yourself. Choose one, though, to help you begin to write.

Make yourself a promise:

I'm going to get my feelings out. I'm not going to be scared. I'm going to write down how I feel each day as I go through this workbook. I'm going to express what I'm discovering, how I'm responding to each new idea, how it helps or doesn't help, where I am right now on the journey. I'll write at least a sentence or two each time I re-read the earlier entries and chapters, because each day is a new day and a new place on the road.

Grief-Recovery Journal

Date _____

Dear _____:

This is how I feel right now:

_____

_____

_____

_____

_____

_____

_____

_____

_____

_____

This is what I've discovered today:

_____

_____

_____

_____

_____

_____

_____

_____

_____

_____

This is what I still question today:

_____

_____

_____

_____

_____

_____

_____

_____

_____

_____

_____

Extra space to finish your thoughts, if needed:

_____

_____

_____

_____

_____

_____

_____

_____

_____

_____

For additional encouragement, listen to
Number 2 on the *Grief Recovery Workbook CD*

Chapter 2

Recovery: Your Roadway Back

During the 1992 school shooting in Olivehurst, California—a hostage situation—we had been called in to work with the assembled parents as they waited to hear whether their sons and daughters would make it out alive. The tension was excruciating as the hours ticked by, but for those parents, the cruel waiting was better than the unwavering truth of a dead child.

A high school dropout had entered the campus with an arsenal of guns. He took eighty-seven hostages and killed three students and a teacher. He negotiated throughout the night and traded lives for pizza and soda. Our primary assignment was to work in the gym with the families who were waiting for their sons and daughters, not knowing whether they were dead or alive.

> Turn your ear to me,
> come quickly to my rescue;
> be my rock of refuge.
>
> *Psalm 31:2*

As the night wore on, hostages would be released and cheers from the relieved family members would fill the gym. This went on half a dozen times until, ultimately, when the last announcement was made, only a few parents were left sitting in the gym. These would become the family members of those who had been killed by the gunman.

I was asked to do the memorial service for about 1,100 students and then return to work with the families on an ongoing basis. The local victim's witness association from the district attorney's office said, "We don't know how to help these kids. Can you help us?" So I committed to going for the next three months to teach interested students, parents, and faculty about the grief process and how to help themselves so they could help others. As I facilitated the community's grieving, I watched the recovery process take place. They taught me what recovery should be and what can hinder its success.

Grief may be a universal human experience, but we don't universally know how to help ourselves deal with it. We don't know how to begin working through the grief process of a loss. And most of us don't have a whole community, school, or organization behind us when personal tragedy strikes to help us toward healthy grieving.

Recently, a little girl told me she was going to Disneyland. A month earlier, her brother committed suicide in their home. When I learned that, I remember thinking, *What would that be like? A little third grade girl who experienced suicide in her home?* If I were her parents, how might I help her grief recovery? Their answer was Disneyland. Her brother's last promise to her was that he was going to take her to Disneyland someday. So the parents decided to take her. That's how this family chose to attempt recovery from their tragedy.

What will it be for you? I can tell you only one thing for certain. Looking at grief can seem to just add to the pain. Very often, the act of dealing with this material brings up feelings that have been suppressed for a long time. It may hurt. The average person's first reaction to pain is to run and hide. Are you feeling like that? You may be tempted to close this workbook right about now.

Please resist.

When you think, *I don't know how much longer I can take this*, that's the time to fasten your seat belt. You haven't gone this far in your personal journey by accident.

I'm about to show you the way to recovery.

It's possible that you may be thinking of the word *recovery* as a negative thing. When you've been ill, you see recovery as becoming well again. "The patient has made a complete recovery," a doctor might say. In the grief process, though, that term doesn't mean exactly the same thing.

Recovery is not a welcome word for some grieving people. In my years of working with survivors of personal, local, and national disasters, I have noticed that when people hear the word *recovery*, they often clam up. Their perception of recovery is forgetting the past, moving forward with a happy face, and never talking about that person again. And they expect that any professional will recommend doing just that.

Or they might equate the concept of recovery with the negative perception of "counseling," which suggests that something is wrong with them mentally or emotionally. That word *counseling* can really push people to the edge. "That's not me. That's for crazy people."

Or maybe recovery seems like an unattainable goal in a far-off land to you right now. Your pain may be so overwhelming, your loss so utterly devastating, that you can't conceive of recovering—of moving back into life again. *I will never recover,* you might be thinking. In fact, some people choose not to recover at all. Why? Usually because they have these kinds of misunderstandings about recovery—misunderstandings that make them stumble before they ever begin the recovery road.

But recovery doesn't mean any of those things in our context. Recovery is not a single event but a process. And the understanding of that difference is all-important in being able to start this next phase, the healthy journey through your loss and onto the road back to life.

So what is recovery, then? Over the years, I've heard many different expressions of confusion about this process:

"How do I know if I'm in recovery?" "How do I know if I am doing what I need to be doing or if I'm stuck?"

Let's define the word within our context. *Webster's* defines *recovery* as "the regaining or reclaiming of a former position." In the grief process, it is that time when we begin to move forward into life again, journeying on the path to discovering new feelings and new understandings about ourselves and our loss. This pathway can be short for some and long for others. But the end of the journey will bring us to a place of comfort and healing.

How do we get started? Let's think back to the image of grief as a wilderness trail like I described in my introduction. On my daily walk of prayer, the path of discovery always takes me to the river, where I experience God in all of his creation. This is a major highlight of my journey, but there is nothing like the final leg. Out of the forest and up the hill, left over the bridge and up the steep slope that takes my breath away, I turn the corner and I am Home! Home to the sounds of padding feet and my dog Buddy greeting me at the door.

That path back to your life is only beginning to be created. And like any journey, you need a good idea of the destination. You need a good grasp of what lies ahead for you and why it's worth the effort to forge that pathway.

I've already mentioned several obstacles to recovery. Let's begin by eliminating some more roadblocks between you and the road back.

ROADBLOCKS TO RECOVERY

On your road to recovery you may come up against certain obstacles that get in the way of most grief recovery efforts. See if you recognize any of these.

Believing That Recovery Means Forgetting a Loved One

One of the main obstacles to taking those first steps onto the road of recovery is, strangely enough, the concept of recovery itself—or more correctly, the misconception of recovery.

"I don't want to feel better, because I don't want to forget."

This erroneous idea is one of the biggest problems I hear when working with people who've experienced traumatic loss. They don't want to recover because they have been conditioned to believe that recovering means forgetting. If they are supposed to forget everything in the past, forget their loved one, store the memory out of sight, then they want nothing to do with the idea.

SELF-CHECK

- Do you want to feel better? If not, why not?

_____

- What is your concept of recovery?

_____

That's not what recovery is. How can anyone possibly say to a mother who has lost a child, "You're going to forget that relationship"? That's cruel in itself. Recovering from grief doesn't mean forgetting. We are not talking about erasing memories. To suggest that God in his infinite wisdom wants us to forget is just not consistent with the heart of God.

Believing the Bad Advice Others Give You

"Don't think about it. Think happy thoughts."

"Life goes on."

"Just get over it."

"Just get a hold of yourself."

"Don't talk about it so much."

"You're dwelling in the past."

"Pull yourself together."

If I had a nickel for every single insensitive remark spoken to a grieving person, I could pay off the national debt! It's almost like some people have grief radar. When you've had a loss, their "duty" is to approach you with a wise, knowing look and then say something totally ridiculous to you. The insensitive comments you will hear can easily hold you back from wanting to recover. They can cripple you before you ever start on the road to recovery.

Most people attempt to alleviate their own awkwardness in the presence of a loss by saying anything that will change the subject. Many will want you to bury your feelings and act okay, even if you aren't, so they won't have to deal with your pain. By force of will, they expect you just to move on and not bother anyone.

Young widows are told, "You're still young, you're attractive; you can just get a new husband." Or a mother who has lost a child will hear: "You can have another child. If you can't have a child, well, you can get a dog." And my favorite: "Be strong for the children. Don't let the kids see you cry." We should mask our grief; hide our emotions from the children, goes this ridiculous train of thought. Why? Because, surely our kids don't really know what's going on. So if we just don't talk about it, if we can stay "strong," it will seem to the kids that nothing is happening.

Does that sound like denial? It is, and it's very unhealthy. Actually, this is one approach that may be the most harmful, not only for you but also for your kids.

Be assured that your children know something is happening. Remaining silent teaches them that they can't talk about their own loss. So your silence will actually teach your children the wrong way to deal with their emotions, much less their grief. It doesn't take long for a child to pick up your behavior. The way we choose to deal with our loss—suppression, denial, hiding it and not talking about it—will be the way our children deal with it.

Believe it or not, part of your recovery is being able to actually understand the impulse behind all these inane comments coming at you. You'll know you are well on the road to recovery when people say such things to you and you don't get upset.

SELF-CHECK

What is the most insensitive thing someone has said to you about your loss?

_____

Why is it ridiculous? _____

Believing That Your Loss Makes You a Loser

Life's true winners are those who have everything, or so we are told. Maybe you lost a child, a job, a relationship, or professional standing. You've lost *something*, so therefore you may feel society sees you as a loser. And nobody wants to be around losers—at least that's what we've been taught since grade school. We are taught to measure our success by what we have. Of course, that's not how God measures our success. But if you believe that your loss somehow makes you a loser, then you may be slow to recover.

This feeling can be painfully enhanced by your friends if they don't know how to respond to your pain. After twenty-five years of marriage, a husband dies, leaving his widow with only a circle of friends who are all couples. And now she is alone, the only widow in the group. She wonders, "Do I still go out to dinner with them? Are they going to feel awkward? Am I?" I've had people in such situations describe the feeling as "anguish" in their hearts. "I not only lost my husband or my wife, but I've lost my whole circle of friends," a woman said to me. The fear that she was subtly seen as a loser compounded her grief.

SELF-CHECK

• Do you feel somehow that your loss makes you a loser in the eyes of the world?

Odds are, you cannot name one person who hasn't lost something in their lives. Does this mean that everyone is a loser and no one is a winner? Or might it mean that part of life is loss, and that at some point everyone loses something, "winners" and "losers" alike?

Believing That Recovery Means Hiding Your Grief

If someone says to you, "How are you today?" odds are, your automatic response would be "Fine."

We have been conditioned by one small social nicety to never really answer that important little question truthfully—at least not with the vast majority of strangers and acquaintances we meet throughout the day who ask us that. You might think that using the phrase "How are you?" as a greeting and not an actual query about your state of health and well-being is just a coincidence. But I don't really think so. I believe it has everything to do with that conditioning. Society expects its citizens to keep a stiff upper lip, to shake it off, to keep on keeping on. It's amazing how we are taught to conceal our grief. After all, no one likes to be around people who have problems, since everyone has enough of their own. Life is so much nicer and easier to handle if everyone will agree to act happy.

Sometimes I tease such people. When they ask the inevitable "How are you?" question, I answer: "Well, my dog died, and my wife just left me, and I've grown another head out of my armpit." But usually it's wasted effort, because they will probably just say, "That's nice," and move on, having heard nary a word.

This is a challenging roadblock to recovery for anyone beginning the grief process. It sends a wrong message—the message that nobody cares, that the best coping mechanism is to just "get over it." Because we are pressured to conceal our grief, then, we feel forced to grieve alone, which can stop the recovery journey in its tracks.

But God has a different plan. God doesn't want you to forget. God doesn't say, "So you've had a loss. So what? So has everybody else." God doesn't say you have to conceal your grief. In his mercy and his compassion, God can be sufficient to meet your needs during this grief process in a unique way that we will outline in the pages to come.

NINE SIGNPOSTS TOWARD RECOVERY

Now that we know how to avoid the recovery roadblocks, what does recovery look and feel like?

Let's look at what lies at the end of your recovery journey. While it may seem impossible at this moment, here's a peek at how you will begin to feel in the weeks and months to come, when you find yourself on the road to recovery:

1. Recovery is feeling better.

We will learn in the pages to come that grief affects us physically, emotionally, and cognitively. You not only have a right to feel all you are feeling, you *need* to feel all you are feeling. You not only have a right to be in a slowed-down state physically and mentally, you *need* to be there. That is your body's way of helping you cope with crisis.

But there is a moment when something changes. And it usually begins with feeling a little bit better than the day before. And that's when you make the choice to take those first steps on the recovery road. Do you want to feel better? Reading these words, working in this workbook—that's your answer to that question, isn't it?

SELF-CHECK

- So, how *are* you?

Your answer (The only wrong answer is "Fine"):

_____

Were you honest? If not, please try again.

_____

2. Recovery is reclaiming your circumstances instead of your circumstances claiming you.

At some point in my seminars, I usually ask this question: "Do you want to gain control of your life again?" There isn't a person on the face of the earth in the midst of grief who doesn't say yes to that question. It's not only the event, but it's the loss of control in almost every aspect of life that can stand in the way of anyone's recovery.

Consider just one area that can feel beyond your control, such as your financial future. After a death, it can involve having to deal financially with the cost of a funeral, or the loss of income from a spouse who is no longer alive to provide. If it's the loss of your job, then that not only affects you financially, but can also strain your marriage. If it's a loss of a relationship, that affects your work, which then affects your income.

The moment you take control of your circumstances instead of letting the circumstances control you, you are showing a sure sign that you are on your way to recovery.

3. Recovery is finding new meaning for living without the fear of future abandonment.

"I don't want to have another relationship because I'm just going to get burned again." That's a statement I've heard many times from people after a devastating loss. "I don't

> "For I know the plans I have for you," declares the LORD, "plans to prosper you and not harm you, plans to give you hope and a future."
>
> *Jeremiah 29:11*

want to have any more children because they're just going to die too," one mother told me. One day, you'll be able to know there is a purpose for your life. You can go on without fear of what tomorrow holds.

Your significance in Christ is not determined by events, circumstances, places, or things. Your circumstances, events—everything—can change, but God doesn't change his purpose or his plan for your life. You'll remember that when you are beginning to recover. As the Jeremiah scripture states, God has a plan for you. And it's good, not evil—it's about the future and hope. That doesn't change.

4. Recovery is being able to enjoy fond memories without having them stir up painful feelings of loss, guilt, and remorse.

There will be a moment when you remember the good times with the person you have lost and you won't feel pain. With God's help and God's plan for recovery, you will. You can remember without all the pain and the anguish. God doesn't want you to forget. The grief process is well on its way when you have coped with your feelings of guilt and remorse to the point that you are no longer focusing on the bad memories to the exclusion of the good.

5. Recovery is acknowledging that it is all right to feel bad from time to time and to be able to talk about those feelings.

Recovery doesn't mean you suddenly announce that you're recovered. It doesn't mean you will never have a bad day. It's acknowledging that it's okay to have a bad day every once in a while, or even a bad week or a bad holiday season. To do so doesn't mean you're not recovering. It just means that you're allowed permission because your grief is unique.

6. Recovery is being able to forgive others when they say or do things that are painful.

As we've discussed, people will say some very dumb things. Sometimes they are intentional, but most often they aren't. When those comments don't have the same sting they once did, when you're able to understand and not take such comments personally, that's a sign you are recovering—you are recognizing what God is doing in your life.

If we don't forgive, we lock ourselves into bitterness, and that causes a vast array of problems for our lives. This is so important that a whole chapter will be devoted to it later. No one is immune to saying the wrong thing, by the way. To prove that point, I want to share a story on myself, when I said the worst possible thing to a grieving widow.

I was working with a woman whose husband had committed suicide by shooting himself. The woman, who wasn't a Christian, was thirty-five years old, and yet she had never written a check or paid a bill. Part of the ministry we have chosen to offer through We Care Compassionate Crisis Care is dealing with the practical needs of victims and survivors due to all the reasons you have just learned. The practical and the physical must be attended to before the emotional needs can be helped. Often our team members have offered to mow lawns and get groceries. Our first priority is to meet people's practical and physical needs as we see them.

This young widow's immediate need was with her finances. I set up an appointment to help her manage her money. I'd had such a full day helping another victim that I was late. I called to tell her so, and the woman graciously said to come whenever I could make it. So finally I arrived, a bit tired and rushed.

She greeted me at the door by asking, "How's your day been?"

Without thinking, I responded: "Well, to be honest with you, I've had one of those days that if I had a gun, I'd shoot myself."

Before you close this workbook in disgust, let me tell you the rest of the story. Let me tell you how God redeems things when we're honest. I, of course, immediately knew what I'd said and how incredibly inappropriate it was. Oh, I knew!

I had a choice to make. I was either going to practice what I preached or I was going to cop out somehow, perhaps act like her grief had made her deaf or forgetful. In counseling, we'd call that "rationalization." But I realized that I had a few seconds of opportunity to redeem myself and the situation—and any further ministry I might be able to offer this woman—by taking responsibility. So I looked at her and said, " I must tell you that in all the years of my ministry—in fact, in all the years of my life—I don't think I've said anything more inconsiderate to anybody. And I would understand right now if you wanted me to leave. With all due respect to you, I ask for your forgiveness."

Her response? This grieving young woman broke into laughter. *Oh no*, I thought. *She's having a nervous breakdown. I really set her off!* But she kept laughing and laughing. So finally I said, "What's so funny?"

"Well, Chaplain Ray," she answered, "you've been helping me so much through the funeral and with all the arrangements these past weeks that my sisters and I were literally beginning to think you were an angel come down from heaven. But because you said something so stupid today, I know that this is not true." And she invited me in. A few years later, I heard from her and she was doing well. I knew she had begun her recovery, though, years before.

7. Recovery is realizing that your ability to talk about your experience helps others coping with their loss.

Some of the best grief recovery material ever written was written by people who have experienced loss. You really know you are recovering when you're able to say, "I've had a loss, and maybe I can share what I've learned with others." Whether it's been recovery from divorce or miscarriage, or from loss to suicide or a drunk driver, the ultimate step of recovery happens when, through all of that pain, you are able to minister to someone else.

After the September 11 terrorist attacks, some of the victims found unique outlets for their grief that helped not only themselves but others in the time-honored, healing ways of community. Two stories reported in the national media during those first post-attack days will forever stay with me. An Oklahoma City man who lost a daughter in the 1995 bombing volunteered to go to New York City to help. Sponsored by the Red Cross, he went, and three times a day he escorted grieving family members on tours of Ground Zero. According to the *Time* magazine account, he felt it was important to show people he was still standing six years later. He had battled depression for three years before controlling it. Going to New York was his way to avoid "getting sucked back into the vortex of grief."

In Washington, D.C., a woman who lost a loved one in the attack on the Pentagon reportedly walked into a nearby coffee shop and paid, in advance, the coffee and dough-nut bill for the soldiers working the cleanup. She found a way to mourn uniquely and healthily by reaching out. The *Life* magazine account of the story recorded the reaction of one Air Force officer: "I have no answers to how someone cultivates a heart as large as that." These stories signaled to me that the event's grief, and its healing promise, had begun.

There is a world out there that is hurting in the same ways you are. "What am I feeling that might help someone else going through the same thing?" Can you answer that? If so, you are on your way to a healthy recovery. If not, don't worry. Make a date with yourself to revisit this page in the days to come. You may not be there yet, and you may not be there for a long time. Every person's journey is different in length. But when you can say that, it is definitely a significant signpost on your recovery road.

Until then, be kind to yourself. And allow others to be kind to you and share their own stories of loss and recovery.

8. Recovery is a return to the desire to live again and provide for the people in your life.

Part of recovery is to have a desire to live again and be concerned about the well-being of those in your care. The opposite is a symptom and a potential result of clinical depression. So after the first few days and weeks of slow, depressive waves, you will find interest in life again. There has to be a "beginning again," especially if you have children. No parent of small children can crawl under the covers and stay in his or her room all day. You'll soon feel that you have to engage the world again. And when you do, even if your children forced you on your feet, you've begun recovery.

SELF-CHECK

- Is there someone you know who wants to share his or her experience with you?

- Are you ready to let them?

9. Recovery is a renewal of faith in God and a rebirth of hope in your life.

Right now you may be angry with God, and an array of emotions may be keeping you from feeling any hope at all. Quite often, this one feeling will be the most painful obstacle to beginning healthy grief recovery. But embracing the truth that God isn't the source of our grief, but the creator of the grieving process put in place for your spiritual health—as well as your physical, emotional, and cognitive health—is another clear sign of recovery. God has always known we would grieve losses, so he created a plan of redemption, a way of hope, to help us cope.

> "I have come that they may have life, and have it to the full."
>
> *John 10:10*

Are your feelings of anger at God creating your largest obstacle in the recovery road? In the pages ahead, we will deal with that anger as well as all the other major emotions of the grief process. For now, just know that recovery offers a return to hope and a better understanding of your faith.

SELF-CHECK

- How many of the recovery steps have you taken yet? All of them? None of them? To begin the journey, it only takes one.

- Which step will be your first?

_____

_____

_____

STARTING THE JOURNEY

Now that you know the roadblocks and you know what your future recovery will feel like, let's start the journey. Let's begin!

1. Admit your need for the journey.

Be honest with yourself about your fears and the reality of your need. Being able to admit needing help is really about getting past the denial that keeps most of us from moving forward.

How is God helping? Have you asked that question? Or have you been too afraid? Perhaps that is part of acknowledging your need in order to begin. Consider making the question a prayer: Ask God, "How are you helping me?" One thing I can assure you, God is ready and available to help you.

2. Be ready to receive tools.

It's one thing to admit that you need to begin the grieving process and to recognize what may hinder your journey, but you need also to learn the "tools" that can help you toward a healthy recovery—and you must use them. It's not good enough just to know they are there; you have to know how to use them.

3. Develop and follow your roadmap.

Another key to a good start is having a plan. Without a map, you can ultimately end up going in circles in your wilderness of grief. When you have a plan, you know where you are starting and you know where God wants you to go.

How do you make a plan? Your decision to work through your own recovery in this workbook is your first step toward that goal. Well done! You not only have a plan, but a personal guide.

In the pages ahead, you are going to acquire the skills and resources you need to journey through your grief. You will venture into the woods and look at the uniqueness of the forest of grief, noting its trees and flowers, shadows and colors and fragrances. You will learn how to manage the guilt, how to alleviate the anger, nurture the forgiveness, cope with the pain, gain perspective on your present responses and your past relationships. Don't be afraid; all the "tools" for the journey will be here in the survival kit. They will not only come from my experience, but also from God's own time-tested resource, the Bible. Think of them as the matches, canteen, pocket knife, and compass that will see you through the wilderness of grief.

Work It Out

1. How far on the recovery roadway are you today?

_____

_____

_____

_____

2. Have you developed a plan with God to process your grief? How do you think God can help you?

_____

_____

_____

_____

3. What resources has God already made available to you to help you with the journey?

_____

_____

_____

_____

4. What resources would you like to have?

_____

_____

_____

_____

_____

Grief Recovery Journal

Date _____

Dear _____:

This is how I feel right now:

_____

_____

_____

_____

_____

_____

_____

_____

_____

_____

_____

This is what I've discovered today:

_____

_____

_____

_____

_____

_____

_____

_____

_____

_____

This is what I still question today:

_____

_____

_____

_____

_____

_____

_____

_____

_____

_____

Extra space to finish your thoughts, if needed:

_____

_____

_____

_____

_____

_____

_____

_____

_____

For additional encouragement, listen to Number 3 on the *Grief Recovery Workbook CD*

Chapter 3

Tools for Your Recovery Road

Mrs. Perez had a very large family. She was a mother of seven and a grandmother several times over. I knew both her and her husband from church. Her husband owned his own landscaping business, and he sometimes ushered with me at the morning services. As happens, Mr. and Mrs. Perez found themselves raising not only their own kids but also, at the same time, their children's kids. The Perezes were working overtime doing all they could to keep their family and extended family together.

One day, Mr. Perez had driven into his driveway with his grandchildren after a long day of landscaping. One was a toddler; some were older. He heard the phone ring and ran into the house to get it, believing that the older children had taken the smaller children into the house with them. But the toddler had fallen asleep and remained in the backseat of the car. It was a summer day in Sacramento, and the temperature was over 100 degrees. The baby asphyxiated before being discovered in the closed car.

> You turned my wailing
> into dancing...
> and clothed me with joy.
>
> *Psalm 30:11*

Mr. Perez was arrested by the police, charged with manslaughter, and jailed over the long Fourth of July weekend. When I received the call, I knew something was just not right with this process. *This man is not a murderer*, I thought as I put down the phone.

He had taken in these kids because he was trying to do the right thing, not because he was trying to kill any of them. This was a man who could have said to the parents of the grandchildren, "I raised you; now go raise your own kids." Instead, he took on a responsibility that proved overwhelming, and it cost the life of his grandchild. Now he was sitting in a county jail. Ultimately, he wasn't charged, but his grandchild had graduated to heaven, and he and Mrs. Perez had to bear the tremendous guilt of that event.

I helped bury the baby and ministered to these two distraught grandparents as best I could. That's when I found out that Mrs. Perez had lost a baby of her own years before. So she and her husband had known grief already—the special grief that comes from a child's death.

But too soon, I received another call for help at the Perez household. The Perezes had lost another child—this time one of their boys. Their son was killed in a drive-by shooting while standing on a street corner. I was with them in the hospital when their son was put on life support. I was there while the whole family came one at a time to say good-bye. And I was there when they had to turn the machines off and watch their son take his last breath.

Mr. and Mrs. Perez's experience could be used to illustrate almost every aspect of the grief process for us—they surely experienced them all. But most of all, what Mrs. Perez taught me is how very unique each loss is. In emotional chaos over the third loss of a child in her family, she finally came to me to talk about it. "When my grandbaby died," she said, " I thought I knew how to do this, to grieve, because I lost my baby daughter so many years ago. But it was different than my daughter. And then when my Junior died, I thought, *I should know how to do this*, but I don't. I can't."

Mrs. Perez can tell you: No matter how many losses you've experienced, you will uniquely grieve every one. Why? Because each loss will be based on the relationship you had with who or what is now gone. And that uniqueness is why specific tools might be needed to help you analyze, as well as manage, your grief process as you move down the road to recovery.

TOOL 1: A PLAN

A plan is basic to beginning your recovery journey. And the easiest way to create a plan is to have a desire or a goal. As you face your unique grief, you can feel alone. The work that lies ahead may seem overwhelming with limited existing resources. Some specific, personal intentions will keep you focused at moments when you might feel yourself wandering.

Look back and review the nine signposts of recovery in the previous chapter. It's important to remind yourself what recovery is, and what you are working toward. The act of writing down important information helps solidify it in your mind. So please list below those nine points—summarizing them in your own words:

Signposts of Recovery

1. _____

_____

2. _____

_____

3. _____

_____

4. _____

_____

5. _____

_____

6. _____

_____

7. _____

_____

8.

_____

9. _____

_____

Now, with your memory refreshed about a proper view of healthy recovery, ask yourself: *What do I want to accomplish through my recovery?* I'll give you a jumpstart. Here are five desires that should be on anyone's list:

Five Desires for Recovery

1. I will accept the reality of my loss. Sometimes when we first lose a loved one, the safest place to be is in denial. So the first step would be accepting the reality of the loss. Living in a suspended state of denial of your reality is a prime breeding ground for emotional, behavioral, and cognitive problems. You don't need any of those. God wants you to live in reality and God wants to help you, so you must accept the reality of the loss.

I recall one woman who finally came to me for help in dealing with her divorce. As the story unfolded, I found out she had nursed her denial for a very long time. She kept telling me, "He's coming back. I know he's coming back to me."

"I'm sorry," I finally said as gently as I could. "You know that he's remarried. He has two kids. It's been five years since your divorce. I don't think he's coming back." We must accept the reality where we find ourselves. That's a strong and all-important goal.

2. I will give myself permission to experience the grief. We will talk about grief—what it looks like, what it feels like, and how you have to give yourself permission to experience that process. That is how you are going to hope again and how you will feel healthy again. The world doesn't allow us to grieve. That's why we must give ourselves permission to walk through the process and not circumvent the journey that God has for us.

It's through the trials and tribulations that we become stronger. As Paul said in his letter to the Romans, who were having quite a few trials and tribulations themselves, such situations are the times in life when we have a chance to truly transform. A loss can be the greatest growth time with God that we will ever experience in our lives. When we want to circumvent the process (and who doesn't want to avoid trials!), and when we hope to live a life of no trials, no storms, nothing but blue sky and rose gardens, we deny ourselves the privilege of having God build character in us.

The alternative—stuffing, suppressing, sweeping your emotions under the nearest rug—only leads to a big mound under the carpet to trip on one dark night. It will be so much harder to deal with ignored emotional reactions to your loss. Make this part of your plan: You have permission to grieve.

3. I need to adjust to my new environment that is minus my loss. A big change has happened to you. For a while, denial of that change is okay; it's a safe place to wait until you are a bit stronger. But it's not a place to build the rest of your life. There is now an absence that must be faced. A worthy goal is learning to adjust to the new environment.

4. I want to reinvest emotional energy. The absence that the loss has created has also created a void in your time. And without a specific desire for refashioning the use of that time, you may flounder for a while. If I were to lose my wife, all of the energy that I spend with her, all the small moments of communication and love that we share, all the joking and kidding, would just stall. I would have to do something with that energy, wouldn't I? Otherwise I would just sit around and talk to myself, which is certainly not a prescription for health, nor a goal for a journey. I have energy to give away and share, somehow, some way. To be open to learning how to reinvest that energy, as God might lead you to do, is a healthy desire.

5. I want to learn how to redefine my roles and relationships. Part of reinvesting your energy is also redefining your roles and relationships without the loved one you lost. A worthy strategy is to consider: What is my new role in my family? In my circle of friends? In my church and my community?

My mother-in-law is a good example of these goals well met. She has changed a lot since her husband died. Their mutual friends are still friends, but she has a different kind of relationship with them now. Seeing her adjust, over the years, into her new role in the world has been interesting. She's reinvested her energy in an admirable way that helps others as well as herself: She runs her church's outreach program to homeless people. To be aware of your need for redefinition is certainly a desired part of your recovery plan.

I've offered five recovery goals to help you begin planning. Your own list may be more specific or more general, and you will want to add more to it as you go along. Below is space for up to five more new desires. Make sure your ideas, however, encompass the signs and the elements of recovery you now know by heart.

6. _____

_____

7. _____

_____

8. _____

_____

9. _____

_____

10. _____

_____

TOOL 2: A LOSS INVENTORY GRAPH

Your second tool, a personalized loss inventory graph, is just what it sounds like. It's personal—meaning it's for you. It's an inventory, and it's done in graph form.

Nothing happens in a void nor by accident. Assessing past losses helps you see how you responded in the past and why you may be responding in a particular way now, after your current loss. That information can instruct as well as comfort you as you move down your recovery road.

Here's how it works. Study the sample of a personal inventory graph offered on the next page. Notice it involves two lines—one vertical, one horizontal. One shows your age and the loss you experienced, and one depicts the intensity of the loss. The zero-to-ten numbering stands for your assessment of the intensity of the pain and its effect on you.

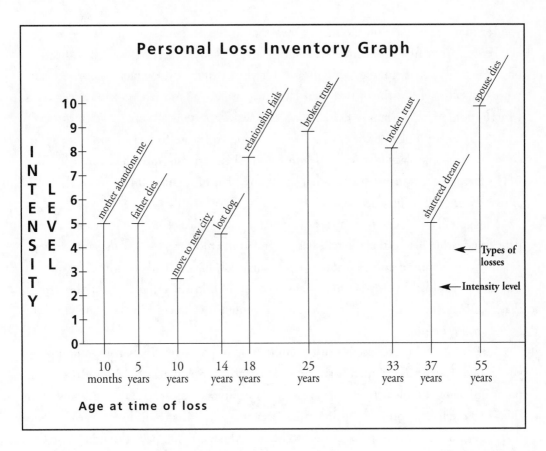

Personal Loss Inventory Graph

How might you gauge the intensity of your loss? Ask yourself how much it hurt. Perhaps you have a childhood memory that will help measure your intensity factor. I was given a Howdy Doody watch and it wasn't shockproof. I'd had it for half a day and, *bang,* I broke the watch. I cried for hours over that one. I wasn't afraid my parents would be mad at me; I was just crushed that I had taken a precious gift they had given to me and already busted it. Now, in looking back, I'd consider that first remembered trauma as having an intensity rating of about a 2 on this graph's scale of 1 to 10.

How far back should you go? As far as you can remember. Jot down the loss, the age, and the intensity of the loss for you. You can make your beginning any loss at the earliest age you can recall.

Perhaps your first loss was like my Howdy Doody watch. Then maybe at the next loss you were ten years old and your parents separated or divorced. Maybe the intensity for you for that loss was a 6 on the scale. Draw that in the next space.

Perhaps your first experience with puppy love in your teen years was a heartbreaking one. You might chart that at perhaps a 4. Or your parents died when you were twenty years old, or maybe at thirty-two your child was stillborn. You felt both were very close to a 10 in intensity. Perhaps you lost a job that was important to you at age thirty-seven, and the intensity might have been a 7. Or maybe you were forced to move across the country, leaving a place you felt was home and all the friends you'd had for years. That might feel like an 8 in intensity. What is the loss that brought you to this workbook? I am sure it should be graphed at a 10.

I suggest using a pencil, because as you begin to list your losses, you will want to compare every earlier loss to the one that has generated the most intensity. You can have many 10s on your graph, of course, though I pray that you haven't had such loss in your life. But more than likely, you will have one or two level-10 losses and others that hover near that number. Allow yourself to reconsider your intensity choices as you create your life's losses on this graph.

The point of this exercise is not to remind you of past pain. In fact, I would not ask you to revisit such painful memories if it did not aid your own healthy grief recovery. The point in having a tool such as a personal loss inventory graph is to show you how many things you've had go on in your life. Whenever you are trying to deal with the emotions that are a product of your loss, it's easy to be overwhelmed. You have thought more than once since your loss, *I'm never going to get over this.* A personal inventory graph is a visual reminder that you can—and you will. You've had other losses; you've prevailed.

But it does one more important thing: It helps you identify losses that you've stuffed or even hidden from yourself. Suddenly, upon studying your own history, you may see something new, some loss you never dealt with that is intensifying your grief today. Eyes wide, you may suddenly think: *There's something I've swept under the carpet and I've been tripping over it for years.*

So first, your graph reminds you of your own strength that has gotten you through past losses. Then, it identifies the losses—some of which you may have stuffed, and some of which you may have repressed, but certainly some that could be getting in your way today. Third, it shows you the intensity of your past losses, which helps you deal with them all.

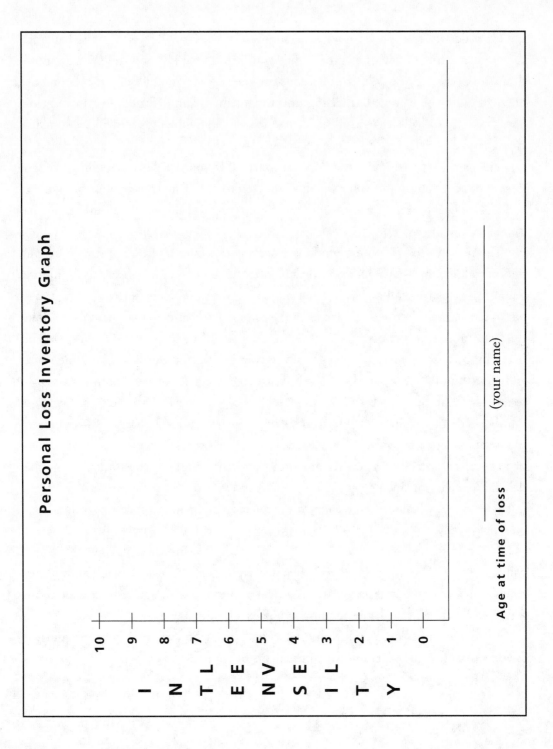

How do you run a marathon? One step at a time. How do you eat an elephant? One bite at a time. How do you deal with your grief? One loss at a time. Don't try to deal with every loss you've ever experienced in one swoop. You will never, ever process anything, and you'll come out feeling nothing but tired and defeated. But I can guarantee you, if you will let God minister to each loss individually, you will see a major change in yourself.

The same is true for the rest of your journey. If you will let God work through your experience ahead—if you will allow yourself to go through each emotion you are feeling one chapter at a time, one day at a time—it will make all the difference in the outcome.

The personal loss inventory graph is especially revealing when we deal with people fighting addictions—drug addicts and alcoholics, sex addicts, eating disorders. With the graph in front of us, I'll ask, "Now tell me where your problems started?" Nine times out of ten, the self-destructive behavior began immediately after a significant loss. Often this is a surprise for the person. "Wow," they'll say, "All these years... Could it be I'm like I am because of what happened?" My answer is always a cautious yes. While some addictions can be related to disease, self-destructive behavior is almost always a manifestation of a deep loss. Most of the time, when you look beyond the behavior, you see unprocessed grief in a person's life. You see where there was a significant loss—a breach of a relationship, a molestation, a broken covenant, a broken promise, the destruction of a marriage, a failure, a job termination—and then you see the onslaught of the destructive behavior. Such people also find grief recovery to be almost cathartic, but definitely exciting, because they recognize their major problem is processing a long-ago grief incorrectly.

This exercise will help you come face-to-face with the various events in your life and will reveal how they might be affecting your current grief process. Remember, nothing happens in a void. A dozen past relationships help you to see how you responded to those events and why you may be responding in a particular way now.

Use this as a reference point from time to time throughout the grief recovery journey as you work through the emotional components of your loss.

PAUSE TO REFLECT

Spend some quality time on the creation of your personal inventory graph. Then take more time to study it. After an in-depth look at your graph, answer some of the following questions. These will help you focus on what you've gained from this tool for the road.

1. "You've had other losses; you've prevailed." Does that sentence reflect one of your responses? If so, why? If not, why not?

_____

_____

_____

2. Did you uncover a loss that you never fully grieved? What is it? How is it possibly still affecting you as you work through your latest loss?

_____

_____

_____

3. How can seeing the intensity of your past losses help you deal with your most intense, latest loss?

_____

_____

_____

TOOL 3: A RELATIONSHIP SURVEY

A relationship survey is designed somewhat the same way as the personal loss inventory graph. This time, though, your starting point is the beginning of the relationship you are now grieving—the loss you have chosen to work through in this workbook.

As we've said, nothing happens in a void. Assessing a past relationship helps you to see how you responded in the past and why you may be responding in a particular way now, after your latest loss. The main idea is to re-create the realistic balance of positive

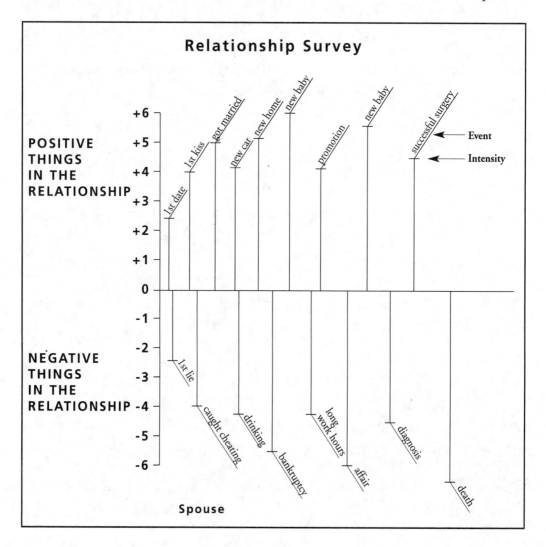

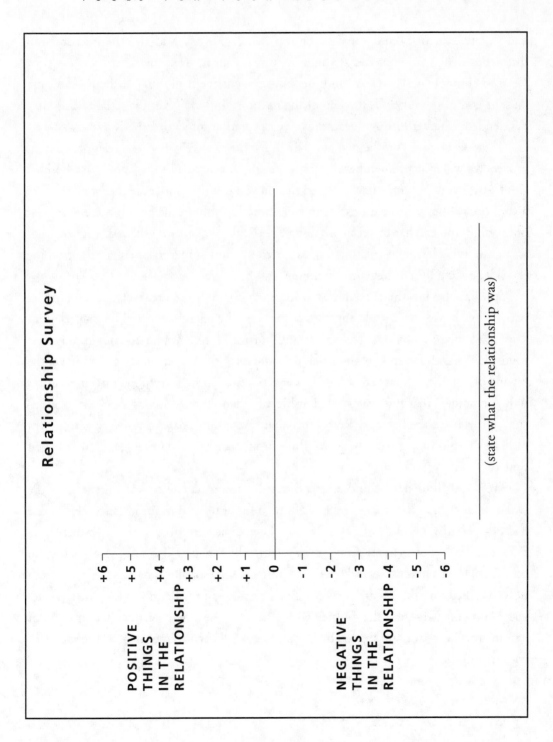

Relationship Survey

POSITIVE
THINGS
IN THE
RELATIONSHIP

+6
+5
+4
+3
+2
+1
0
-1
-2
-3
-4
-5
-6

NEGATIVE
THINGS
IN THE
RELATIONSHIP

(state what the relationship was)

and negative factors about the relationship being grieved. And that information can instruct as well as comfort you as you move down your recovery road.

The chronological starting point on this survey is the beginning of the relationship, and the end of the survey is the end of the relationship—however that relationship may have ended, whether through death, divorce, separation, or some other way.

There seems always to be two radically different ways we will view a relationship that is over. We will either remember every good thing or every bad thing, but rarely both. Is this true for you? You may have noticed that all you can remember are the wonderful (or awful) things about the relationship. In fact, everything about the person was either great or horrible. You can hardly recall anything else. Reality gets a little skewed. Your off-center perspective may be re-creating the lost loved one into a martyr or an angel, or on the flip side, casting him or her into subhuman status.

So what does creating a relationship survey do for your grief recovery? It can put you back in touch with reality, placing correct focus on the relationship. All human relationships are a mixture of wonderful things and hurtful things. A married couple can point to many wonderful events in a normal life—the birth of a child, starting a business, the buying of a home. A married couple can also point to some incredibly hurtful events as well—reminders that this was a relationship that had failures. It was a *human* relationship. Do you see the balance? Remember that one of our goals in recovery is to accept reality. A relationship survey helps to bring people back to a state of reality about their time together.

I've heard those left behind after a bitter divorce articulate the deep belief that the whole relationship was terrible and had always been terrible. But, for instance, the couple had three healthy, normal kids. How could it have all been terrible? Obviously, there were some good times, worthy of remembering correctly. We can't live outside of reality, no matter what the circumstance. The past, with its balance of all human experience, needs to be honored for your own peace of mind. The survey provides a focal point by which you can proceed through the journey with a healthy assessment of the relationship that you are grieving—not one skewed by all positives or all negatives, as may be the case with your memories.

TOOL 4: ACTIONS TIMELINE

Depending on the type loss you have experienced, you may also want to use the services of a timeline tool. This is extremely helpful in dealing with guilt, as you'll see in the pages ahead, but can also be used with any other emotion that may be distorting your memory of events and your participation in them.

During a long illness or hospitalization, I often encourage loved ones to keep a diary or journal of the process, recording all the actions taken for the loved one—all the trips to the doctor, all the changing of bed linens, all the medication-giving, all the long nights, all the services rendered to the loved one and the things endured—to help with the guilt that will inevitably follow.

During the grief recovery effort to come, a timeline can be almost as helpful in bringing the experience and your participation in it back into proper perspective. After a death, you may obsess over the time you couldn't take off from work to chauffeur the loved one to a doctor's appointment and also forget all the other dutiful, loving services you performed. "Did I do enough?" "Did I let her down?" "Could I have prevented his pain?" All these questions and more will come tiptoeing through your mind in the quiet hours after a tragedy. This tool can help.

Look at the sample timeline. Refer to it to help you complete the blank one. On the

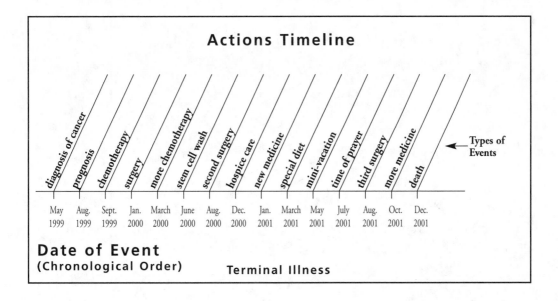

Actions Timeline

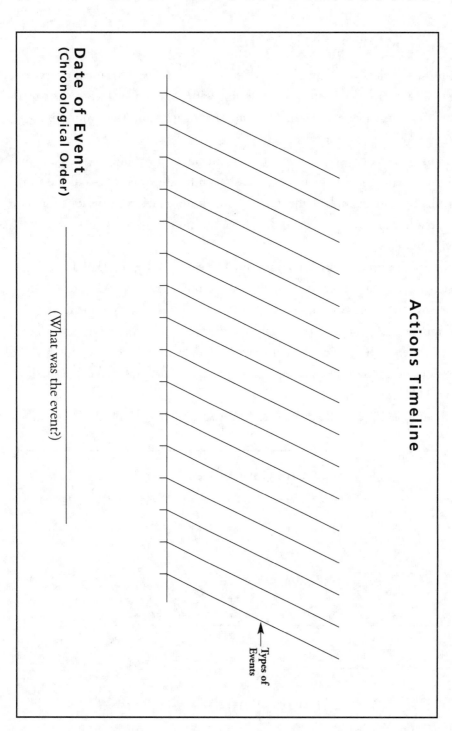

Types of
Events

Date of Event
(Chronological Order)

_____

(What was the event?)

horizontal line is the amount of time that passed. You might need for it to be in increments of days, weeks, or years. If so, add whatever type of information is needed to make it work for you.

Then along the vertical lines, jot down the things you recall. This is a universal sort of tool that can be recalibrated to fit your need. What it should ultimately offer you, of course, is a reminder of your faithful behavior during a difficult time. Make it suit your needs. Your timeline could be a chart of your triumphs over your anger day to day or week to week during your recovery efforts, or it could even be full of reminders of God's faithfulness during your grief process that might help strengthen your faith.

> "But when he, the Spirit of truth, comes, he will guide you into all truth."
>
> *John 16:13*

As more memories come to mind, add them to your timeline. Soon you'll have a tool that has propelled you along on your grief recovery even as you've been creating it.

TOOL 5: YOUR FAITH IN GOD

Your last tool is really both your first and your last—and it fuels all the tools in between: your faith in God and his wisdom. You will use this tool in the remainder of this workbook to obtain God's perspective of your grief recovery, which is the center of the entire effort. It is the baseline source of all other tools for managing our grief. Or to use another metaphor, God isn't just one of the spokes on the wheel. God is the hub. All other tools are just spokes that will help you along the journey. He has created the grief process, after all, so he knows what we need.

More often than we think, great times of loss are also potentially great moments of deepening faith. This is so often true that I believe it is meant to be part of the grief process. Not only is God all-knowing and all-powerful, but God is present everywhere. That's the part of his character that I appreciate most.

I was adopted as a young child by a couple who loved me very much. But I remember how busy my adopted father always was. He was a military man during most of my childhood, and as anyone knows, that can take a father away from his family more than the normal job. So it was very special to me to learn that God the Father is always present, always available, always there. That belief alone can propel you forward in a healthy way. But there is much more.

Three basic aspects of faith in God are vital as tools in the context of your grief recovery and the work you are doing here.

First, your faith in God opens you to a very special comforter and teacher who is always with you. When Christ left the disciples to return to heaven, he told them they would never be alone. He talked of a Comforter who would help them discern truth, guide them, and indwell them. In other words, he describes God in a form our Christian faith understands as the Holy Spirit, the third member of the Trinity. This scripture passage is discussing what I humbly call a tool for grief recovery. God sent the disciples—and he sends us—the Comforter. Why? Because he knew that we would need to be divinely loved and divinely led into truth. Christian theology teaches that the Holy Spirit is God within us who helps us respond to life from the God's-eye view. With him we are able to cope and to experience a peace that passes understanding.

> Rejoice with those who rejoice; mourn with those who mourn.
>
> *Romans 12:15*

Second, there is the Bible. The Bible is a collection of stories about people in need. And that's why it is such a good guide for living, even beyond the gospel of Christ. Not only do we have God as a resource, but we also have his Word. That seems to have been part of its mandate for the human race over two millennia—a roadmap for our journey.

In the pages ahead, I will lead you to consult this roadmap so you may acquire the God's-eye view that you need to complete a healthy grief recovery. Even if you are feeling anger toward God for your loss, the answer to that anger can be understood through this tool. You will discover what the scriptural truth has to say because, as Christ himself told us, it's the truth that sets us free.

Third, a resource tool of incredible help to any grief recovery is the body of Christ, and I can only hope you will have a chance to use it as well. Who is the body of Christ? We are. Not a building or the chairs but the people—fellow Christians everywhere. It's the family of God. And a grieving person needs the encouragement the family of God can offer.

At the close of my seminar several years ago, I spoke at length to two women I had gotten to know during the classes. Ten minutes later, they were in a car accident; one was killed and the other badly injured. I visited the surviving woman in the hospital and asked, "How are you?"

"I'm just so thankful that I have the family of God, my church friends, around me at this time," she answered. When a catastrophe in life strikes, the church should move into high gear. It should be there to lift up and encourage. Christians should be just as good at weeping as we are at singing and sermonizing and laughing, as faithful at funerals and bedsides as weddings and home fellowship groups. Look at your family of God as a tool. We, other Christians, should always be there for you.

Work It Out

You have five tools essential to the grief process.

Take a hard look inside before going into the deep issues ahead. Some of these questions will evoke a little bit of pain along with a little bit of thought. Take the time to really think about that reality, and express it alongside your answer or in your journal pages that follow.

1. What changes in your environment and relationships can you expect as a result of your loss?

   _____

   _____

   _____

2. What role will God play in these changes?

   _____

   _____

   _____

3. Does anything stand in the way of seeking God's help? How about your own anger? The response, or lack thereof, of the church as we've described it? Your lack of Bible knowledge?

_____

_____

_____

_____

4. How do you see these tools assisting you through your journey of grief? Which ones will help your specific situation most? Which tools need sharpening?

_____

_____

_____

Grief Recovery Journal

Date _____

Dear _____ :

This is how I feel right now:

_____

_____

_____

_____

_____

_____

This is what I've discovered today:

This is what I still question today:

_____

_____

_____

_____

_____

Extra space to finish your thoughts, if needed:

_____

_____

_____

_____

_____

_____

_____

_____

_____

For additional encouragement, listen to Number 4 on the *Grief Recovery Workbook CD*

Chapter 4

Grief: What Is It?

Sean was seventeen years old, a junior in high school. One evening, he and some friends went for a walk. One of the boys tossed a bottle over a mound in the road's median. It almost hit a passing car. The car stopped, the passengers jumped out, and within seconds, Sean lay dead from a knife wound.

Todd was also seventeen and a junior in high school. One day, while he was visiting at a friend's house, the friend showed him a rifle. The rifle discharged and Todd was shot in the chest, dying shortly afterwards.

> "Come to me, all you
> who are weary
> and burdened,
> and I will give you rest."
> *Matthew 11:28*

These two deaths happened very early in my years as a crisis chaplain. Listening to the boys' family members and friends, and especially to their mothers, I learned quickly that every idea I had about the grief experience needed to be rethought.

I learned that no pat answers, especially pat religious answers—pray more, trust God more, believe more—worked; in fact, they caused further pain. As the days went by and I watched and listened and grieved along with all the people who loved these two boys, I began to form a hands-on, real-life definition of my own. What I heard stretched the boundaries of any concept of grief I'd ever been offered. These friends and families would talk about feeling physical pain, nausea, body ache. They would talk about the emotions they couldn't control.

One mother described her grief in terms of an ocean. She felt she was caught in the surf, trying to get to dry land, while the waves kept crashing in on her, tumbling her into the sand. Every time she felt as if she had gotten her balance, an undertow knocked her back into the water. As Sean's mother was telling me this story at her kitchen table, she'd smile and then laugh as she caught the memory of her son; then she'd pause, reflect on another thought, stop, and begin to cry as she realized once more that he was gone and she would not see him again.

Todd's mom described her experience as being trapped on an emotional roller coaster ride. She would sit on her living room couch and tell me how much it would hurt one second, and then nothing. A roller coaster ride: up and down, up and down, happy memory, sadness, emptiness, anger and rage, back to numbness—and the cycle starts all over again.

And then there were the specific target emotions that were fueled by personal issues. Sean's mother internalized her pain. Privately she harbored lots of guilt and felt personally responsible, like she hadn't done enough. She should have protected her "baby" more. Todd's mother felt anger towards the senselessness of the act and the justice system's response.

Observing these two mothers convinced me that grief is definitely a process. No chicken soup could soothe their suffering. It was going to take time. I've watched these mothers work through their grief for years: through the first anniversary of their sons' deaths; through the dates the boys would have graduated; through the release dates of the sons' killers. It has been a very hard recovery road for these women, and they will live with the events and journey through the process for a lifetime to come.

Watching both mothers also convinced me that each individual's loss creates a unique grief response. Two young boys, two beautiful mothers, yet the grief was very different. The same was true with all the other family members as well as the boys' hundreds of friends. Sean's father wanted to talk all the time, deeply concerned about the impact of the events on others, especially children. His daughter lost a brother but also was in danger of losing a mother who was isolating herself and a father who was trying to hold it all together. Todd's sister lost a brother she loved so deeply that seemingly nothing would heal her pain.

I had to rethink grief and come up with a better definition. After listening to these people and hundreds of others, I came to develop my own definition of grief that would explain what I'd seen and heard. The result was a concept in which grief was not something to scorn or avoid, but a process to be embraced.

The two mothers are friends today, all these years later. One of the boys' fathers went on to be one of the first participants in the grief recovery class and helped facilitate with other dads and moms who had lost their children. And now they are all helping me help you. They have taken their own personal journeys through the forest, finding healing, and so will you.

A SIMPLE DEFINITION OF GRIEF

Attempting to define grief is like trying to hold on to Jell-O. Everybody knows what it feels like, and sometimes they recognize what it looks like, but to define it or talk about it is very difficult.

Mental health experts talk of the "stages" of grief, but I've noticed that people take that concept too literally, thereby short-circuiting its value. Why does the idea of stages not exactly fit for grief? Sean and Todd's mothers knew—the process seems more an ocean, the waves moving you back and forth, down and up, and then down again.

"Stages" suggests a steady movement from one place to another. In grief you will often think, *I thought I was already at the stage of acceptance, but here I'm back to not thinking clearly again. What's going on?*

Two steps forward, one step back is really the best we can ever hope for as we keep struggling to move down the wilderness road. So I want to offer you a different definition of grief formulated over years of crisis counseling. A definition which has been born out of the hardship and loss endured by two mothers. Then we'll break it down into segments as we work through it.

Grief is the normal process of natural emotions and feelings which are uniquely experienced after any loss of any relationship.

This definition is packed with important words, and there's nothing better than a visual to fix something important in your mind. So, to start our examination of grief in a memorable way, take a highlighter or colored pen and mark the following six words in the definition above:

normal

process

natural

emotions

uniquely

any

Let's look closely at each of the definition's most important words. Fill in the blank with the missing word as we go:

1. GRIEF IS NORMAL

Grief is the _____ process of natural emotions and feelings which are uniquely experienced after any loss of any relationship.

First, grief is normal. It's part of life. It's unavoidable and is going to happen to you sooner or later. It's an automatic thing. A professional way to put it is that grief is innate. It's built in to us. It's normal for each and every human being to grieve. It doesn't depend on your upbringing or your environment. It doesn't depend on how rich or poor you may be.

> We do not want you...to grieve like the rest of men, who have no hope. We believe that Jesus died and rose again and so we believe that God will bring with Jesus those who have fallen asleep in him.
>
> *1 Thessalonians 4:13-14*

Does it make a difference if you're a Christian? Yes, but not as much as you might think. I've heard some people express a hyper-faith mentality that believes mourning isn't faith, that grieving somehow shows a lack of faith. It goes something like this: "Because we are Christians, we should always be happy, never sad, and certainly never grief-stricken. Why, if you just had enough faith, you wouldn't be hurting."

You've probably heard someone say this. The problem with this mentality is that it doesn't work. Attempting to live up to that idea will only make you feel guilty about not being a good enough Christian. In reality, it can actually drive people away from their faith.

We will grieve because the grief process is built in to our bodies, but by using Scripture as our reference, we have the opportunity to process it differently. Why? Because we have a different perspective. Christians have hope.

2. GRIEF IS NATURAL

Grief is the normal process of _____ emotions and feelings which are uniquely experienced after any loss of any relationship.

Grieving is normal and natural—it's not artificial. We live in physical bodies. Because we have this physical body, we are physical people and will respond in a physical way to almost every event in our lives. Think about it. Jesus Christ was 100 percent human and 100 percent divine, and he grieved.

Grief is natural. It will occur with any loss you experience. Why? Because our bodies are created in such a way to help process the loss. God provides our bodies with a dose of adrenalin to help us cope. The chemicals in our brain actually slow down with any shock to the system, allowing us to take in the loss we have experienced. That's how wonderfully God crafted our bodies. Your inability to articulate sentences, to complete a thought, or to eat a full meal is a normal, natural response which enables you to absorb the loss, especially if it's been particularly traumatic.

> Jesus wept.
>
> *John 11:35*

We don't have to be afraid of grief. We don't have to run from it; we don't have to stuff it and pretend like it's not happening; and we don't have to be embarrassed by it. Everybody will experience grief, and that tells us that we are not alone. To hear that everybody feels like this is almost always the first good news for a person going through a loss. And it's true. People lose their appetite. Some can't remember their loved one's name and important dates. You're not going crazy; you're responding naturally.

PAUSE TO REFLECT

Repeat after me:

- God created my body and mind to be able to cope with and assimilate the loss.
- Although I may feel like it, I am not losing my mind.
- I am not alone. God and others are here to assist me.

3. GRIEF IS A PROCESS

Grief is the normal_____ of natural emotions and feelings which are uniquely experienced after any loss of any relationship.

Grief is normal, it's natural, and it's a process. Because it's a process, it will involve many changes. You must give yourself permission to experience each of them.

One woman I worked with immediately following her husband's death could barely talk. All she did was sit there, saying the same thing over and over again. She couldn't get her thoughts together. She would cry and cry and cry. I could tell she wanted to express her feelings, yet she just couldn't think straight enough to do so. For her first ten sessions, all she could do was repeat the same story. Had the woman sought help with someone who didn't understand this aspect of grief, she and the listener could have been very frustrated.

Grief comes in waves; it's not one act that will suddenly end. And we need to give ourselves permission to go through that process, to lie back into the waves and float with them. Sometimes the waves of the grief process are sudden. You can get up in the morning and think, "I'm going to have a great day," then walk into the kitchen, make coffee, and be reminded that your husband was the one who always had the coffee already brewing. Or maybe it will be opening the cabinet and finding your wife's favorite mug or just passing by your son's room who is no longer there. Your day can literally go from the sky to the gutter, triumph to defeat, in a matter of seconds.

A woman I was counseling whose husband committed suicide found this to be true in a dramatic way. One day, she was feeling good enough to leave the house. She opened the door to the garage, saw the car in which her husband committed suicide, and woke up in the hospital. She had fallen down the steps, knocking herself unconscious. That's how quickly the changes can come.

How long will your grief process take? That's the question everyone asks. My answer: Nobody knows. Our modern culture has acquired an unhealthy view of grief, thinking it can be controlled, that it's a thing that we can and should get over quickly: We've got to get rid of the body, get past the funeral, get over it all, and get back to work. We are encouraged to see grief as a Band-Aid, not a process. You will invariably be rushed through the process, and you will have to fight that mentality. The average time any employer will allow you after a death in the family, for example, is three days. But if survivors and victims' families aren't given permission to grieve, they'll develop what we call "chronic grief." They'll get stuck in the first part of the process and never move forward.

Consider the ramifications of certain members of society being rushed through grief. Let's say you're a bank teller, and you just lost your father and mother in an automobile accident. You're responsible for massive amounts of money, and yet you will be expected not to let one penny stray, even if your mind strays. Or what if you're a nurse and you have to distribute medicine to those in your care? You have to make sure you do all your duties safely, that you don't put eyedrops in ears and eardrops in eyes; you have to make sure you don't give the wrong pills to your patients. Or what if you carry a gun in your line of work, such as a police officer, and after three days you aren't quite thinking straight, but you are back working with the public? Could you imagine returning to work in three days in those situations?

Now take that scenario home. How many days do you get off if you've had a separation in your family? None. And how about for a divorce? None. And what if you have small children? Can you hurry your grief in order to care for them?

We live in a society desensitized to death, grief, and loss. And yet if you do not permit yourself to experience grief as a process, you are in danger of finding yourself in a chronic grief state, stuck in unhealthy responses to your future. Nobody is going to give you permission. So it's important that you give it to yourself and walk through the process slowly, deliberately, healthily.

SELF-CHECK

Writing down what you learn is a proven way of remembering it. Fill in the following blanks as best you can:

- God's purpose of the grieving process is to remind you to _____.

- How long do you think your grief process will take? _____.

4. GRIEF IS A TIME OF EMOTIONS

Grief is the normal process of natural _____ and feelings which are uniquely experienced after any loss of any relationship.

Grief is comprised of complex, conflicting emotions, and they seem to come and go at will. Sometimes the waves of emotion ebb and flow from day to day, sometimes week to week, and sometimes month to month. But at the beginning of your grief process, it will seem minute to minute. You can go from feeling good to crying hysterically in an instant.

But why do we have emotions in the first place? I have always seen emotions in an image—my car's dashboard and all its warning lights. For three months a warning light was lit on my dashboard, but because it was visible only at night I just pretended it was illuminating my dashboard. I acted as if it wasn't there, but someday a police officer was going to remind me that it was there because my right headlight was out. Because I didn't drive that car frequently, I didn't get around to fixing it for some time. But of course when I did have the repair done, the dashboard light turned off.

Emotion's role in the grief process is like that image. Each strong emotion you feel is an indicator of need. For example, when you are afraid, those feelings of fear are telling you something. They should force you to consider what you need to do to turn that light off. Each strong emotion can signal a need to focus on God's power, peace, love, enlightenment, and all the aspects of a healthy spiritual life.

Some people suppress their emotions, pretending the dashboard light isn't flashing. But we ignore the dashboard lights at our own peril. Others don't suppress, they express—all the time. Whichever one you are, neither approach works for long. The older you are right now, the more you will suppress. That's because most older adults were taught growing up that suppression was good. But with the wide acceptance of professional counseling in the last few decades, we have been taught that the way to handle strong emotions is to "vent." Remember "scream therapy?" It didn't last long. The reason is, you still feel the same way, don't you? Just a little more hoarse, perhaps.

Venting doesn't solve the matter and suppression doesn't solve the matter. So, since God built these strong emotions into the package, what must you do with them? We will discuss this further in the pages ahead, but right now, think about these ideas for action:

Acknowledge to God that you are feeling this emotion, and then attempt to understand what the "flashing light" is signaling about your need.

Ask: "What is God wanting to teach me through this emotion?" Remember, God's purpose for the grief process is ultimately to lead us to a relationship with him. God wants to use every situation, whether good or bad, to grow us toward the abundant life spoken of in Scripture.

5. EACH GRIEF IS UNIQUE

Grief is the normal process of natural emotions and feelings which are _____ experienced after any loss of any relationship.

During my months of work in New York City following the World Trade Center disaster of September 11, 2001, I spent days and days helping the students, teachers, and staff of a community college within sight of Ground Zero cope with their trauma.

SELF-CHECK

- What emotions are you feeling right now?

_____

- What dashboard lights have been on during the last twenty-four hours?

_____

Three students—two sisters and a boyfriend—who came to me one day are unforgettable. They demonstrated, as clearly as I've ever seen, the truth that grief is as unique as the individual. Even when the loss or catastrophe experienced is the same, the responses can be vastly different.

The older sister was the reason they were there. She wanted to talk, her sister didn't, and the boyfriend wanted nothing to do with us. He was only along because his girlfriend had forced him to come.

The older sister handed me a snapshot of a friend who'd earned an internship at a Twin Towers company and was now missing. When the first plane hit, she said, the three of them had been outside their school. As they were standing there, staring at the fire above them, the second plane hit, and they watched as people fell to their deaths.

Thinking how horrific this must have been for such young eyes, I had to ask, "Did you see those people hit the ground?"

Mercifully enough, there was a building obstructing their view. "We could see them falling, and then nothing." But she still felt guilty. "Why didn't I look away?" she asked.

Then the first tower collapsed, and they ran for their lives.

I glanced at the boyfriend sitting sullenly next to the two sisters. He looked as if he wanted to run from this conversation just as fast as he had run from the dust cloud that day. The older sister began to goad her younger sister into talking, but she refused. "Why do I want to talk about it?" she kept saying. Finally, she admitted, all but stuttering, "I can't talk about it because I don't know how to! How can I possibly tell you . . . what words could I even . . . I just can't!"

What words can I tell you to describe what I'm feeling? That's what she was saying. Her response is one often experienced by young survivors. Adults assume that if small children affected by a disaster are safe and quiet, they are fine. But the truth is, they haven't developed a vocabulary to express their emotions. And these students were still children, no matter what they might have said to the contrary.

The students were three human beings trying to figure out their grief. They reacted in the ways most people do to personal loss—some don't want to talk about it, some do, and some say, in effect, "Let me get away; let me deal with it in my own way. Let me go punch a wall so I don't hurt anyone."

The three students, having experienced the same trauma, responded three different ways. What does that mean for you?

Although you are handling your own grief, you will also be forced to interact with others around you who have been affected by the same loss. Your marriage or family is going to be under great stress during the same time you are working through your grief process. The potential for damage to all these relationships is large if you don't also allow others to grieve in their own ways and times. Again, the process is unique and demands the time it demands—and nothing less—for each individual. We are uniquely made in God's image. Likewise, our relationships are unique—and so will be our reactions to loss.

I see this problem most tragically in marriages. The most common error people make is substituting what they're feeling for what their spouse is feeling. When you assume that your spouse is feeling what you are, and you get mad at him or her for not feeling the same thing, you're headed for big problems. If you force your spouse to process emotions the way you do, you will have yet another loss in your life as you watch that relationship slowly die.

Let me give you an example. When the loss in a family is a child, almost 70 percent of the marriages fail within the first year because spouses do not grasp that their mates are grieving in altogether different ways. That makes the situation ripe for misunderstanding and conflict. The couple can't help each other when they don't understand how very different their reactions can be.

You can even be an expert in the field, a compassionate crisis care professional, and still be susceptible to this dynamic. I know from experience. My wife and I have had two miscarriages. When the first one happened, I totally missed the emotional pain that Cathy experienced. I asked about her health. That's literally all I was worried about. Was she okay physically? When she answered yes, then I was on to the next subject. We didn't talk about it; I didn't skip a day of work; I didn't cancel a counseling session; we didn't miss a beat. It wasn't until we had the second miscarriage that I processed this loss in a whole different way. I finally grasped what a true loss the experience was for her—and for me—and asked Cathy what she was feeling. And this time I wasn't just inquiring about her physical health. I took time off, and we talked a long time about it all.

The marital grief dynamic of losing a child is intriguing. The wife grieves into the past; the husband grieves into the future.

She will express her loss by talking of memories—"I remember when my child was conceived. I remember when he was born. I remember when she first kicked. I remember when she first called my name . . ."

The father, though, grieves the loss into the future. He will talk of hopes and dreams—"I'm going to miss seeing her go to high school. I wanted to teach him how to drive a car." Most often, though, he won't express those dreams; he'll suppress them. The wife then can't understand why her husband won't talk about it. The husband complains that is all she wants to do—talk about the past. Men also have a tendency to rush the process or work overtime to hide from the process. Meanwhile, the wife is left to deal with the loss all alone.

Each loss can create a different grief process too. Remember Mrs. Perez, the grandmother who lost three children over the period of her adult life? Her first loss was a daughter who died a crib death. Her second loss, a grandson, died from accidental heat over-exposure. The third child was shot on a street corner. It would seem that we could have treated each one of those losses in her life the same way. It wasn't so. During the first loss, she felt guilt. When she told me that, I suggested we focus on her guilt for her grandson's and son's deaths. But as she explained, guilt wasn't an emotion she was feeling at all in these later losses. She felt only anger over the shooting death of her son. When I asked if she felt anger over her grandchild's death, her answer was surprising, even to her. For the second loss, she felt loneliness most of all. She felt like God had abandoned her, and that made her feel hopeless and helpless. One woman, three losses, three unique responses to each and every loss.

God deals with us as individuals, knowing our unique needs. There is no magical standard; God looks at you individually, personally. That's why we don't put time frames on how long a grieving process is going to take. Will it be three to six months? A year? We can't tell you that—it's unique to you. Even ten years down the road, something may trigger some emotion connected to the loss.

Grief is so unique that it can't be taken away. Even doing this workbook will not take away your grief. But it will help you move through its process in a healthier way. In time, when that emotional memory triggers your old grief ten years from now, it will be a small effect, and hopefully, a life-affirming one.

6. GRIEF COMES FROM ANY LOSS

Grief is the normal process of natural emotions and feelings which are uniquely experienced after _____ loss of _____ relationship.

Grief is created from any loss, no matter its "importance." It comes in all forms from all origins. The grief that occurs over any loss of any relationship is always different, yet always real. You will be surprised at the depth of feeling you'll have with small losses as well as big ones. And we can easily allow the losses to pile up so high that when one of the seemingly "bigger" losses happen, a domino effect can occur. Daily we are open to loss, and any loss can trigger a response which we call grief. As we mentioned earlier, the grief process cannot be eliminated. It is part of the way we are made. And our daily lives will create many losses that produce our grief response. The only question is: Will you go through these feelings in a healthy or unhealthy way?

CHOOSE ONE LOSS

I love to travel with my wife, but I can honestly say that I don't like all the luggage. *Do we really need all this stuff?* I often find myself asking. My advice is: When taking a trip, pack light. Likewise, don't try to take all the losses in your life and cope with them collectively as you're going through this journey on the pathway through grief. Processing all those losses in one workbook experience is self-defeating. So give yourself permission just to work on that loss that is causing you the most pain right now, knowing that you can return to the forest as often as you need to in order to deal with each and every loss.

Choose that loss as your focus for this workbook. Apply all that you are going to experience to that loss. Then you'll find that it will trickle down into your other losses as well—as you make it part of your continuing journey of recovery.

SELF-CHECK

❧

• Choose one loss for this workbook's focus, the one that compelled you to read this far.

Name that one loss. _____

Work It Out

1. What is the brightest warning light on your emotional dashboard?

_____

_____

_____

_____

2. Where is God in this picture? Do you see God as part of your healing or part of your grief at this moment?

_____

_____

_____

_____

3. What would you like God and others to do for you to help you through this time?

_____

_____

_____

_____

4. How is the loss uniquely affecting those around you: your spouse, your children, your friends?

_____

_____

_____

_____

Grief Recovery Journal

Date _____

Dear _____:

This is how I feel right now:

_____

_____

_____

_____

_____

_____

_____

_____

_____

_____

_____

This is what I've discovered today:

_____

_____

_____

_____

_____

_____

_____

_____

_____

_____

This is what I still question today:

_____

_____

_____

_____

_____

_____

_____

_____

_____

_____

_____

Extra space to finish your thoughts, if needed:

_____

_____

_____

_____

_____

_____

_____

_____

_____

_____

_____

For additional encouragement, listen to
Number 5 on the *Grief Recovery Workbook CD*

Chapter 5

How Does Loss Affect You?

During the lunch hour at a Luby's cafeteria in Killeen, Texas, in 1991, a deranged man, upset with his girlfriend, drove his car through the restaurant's plate-glass window. When one of the diners rushed over to see if he was okay, thinking it was an accident, he was shot dead. The gunman then summarily executed every woman in the restaurant who remotely resembled his girlfriend. Before he turned the gun on himself, twenty-two people who were just having their lunch died that day on the restaurant floor.

> Be merciful to me,
> O LORD, for I am in
> distress; my eyes grow
> weak with sorrow, my
> soul and my body
> with grief.
>
> *Psalm 31:9*

As the national news reported this, the nation was in shock. Mass shootings were unheard of at the time. Many crisis professionals immediately traveled there, including our We Care team, part of our newly organized compassionate crisis care ministry. We got there within twenty-four hours of the shooting. The climate was so chaotic that all the bodies hadn't even been removed from the scene yet. The smell of gunpowder and blood within the shattered restaurant was overpowering. The drama that went on in those long minutes between the time the man drove into the cafeteria's window and the time he aimed the gun at himself began to be told. The story to come—that of the event's impact on the community—was only beginning.

Killeen, the central Texas town known best for its proximity to Fort Hood, the U.S. Army base, received enormous attention as well as substantial emergency intervention and funds. Such organized national response was still very new, and the result of such inexperience was more than a little confusion. Then I happened to hear that the majority of those killed in the cafeteria that day were from a tiny town on the outskirts of Killeen called Copperas Cove. While all the national attention and emergency services had been focused on Killeen, Copperas Cove had been all but overlooked. So after contacting the town's mayor to offer our services, we were invited to set up an emergency counseling center in one of its largest churches. The town's officials spread the word that crisis chaplains from California were waiting to talk to anyone who needed to talk, all free of charge.

We assigned one of our team members to find the surviving family members to make sure each one had some sort of contact with crisis help. The rest of us began talking to the hundreds of townspeople who came to the church. The entire community, it seemed, was showing signs of being affected in unusual ways. They spoke of their loss of appetite, their fatigue, their nightmares, their physical pain as well as emotional traumas. Over and over, people asked the same questions: "Why don't I want to eat? Why can't I sleep? What's wrong with me?"

"I don't know, but we'll find out," I answered.

Doctors, lawyers, gas station attendants, school teachers—a community of people from every socio-economic and cultural class—were experiencing the physical effects of loss. And not only were the town's adults scared and nervous themselves, they needed advice on how to handle the secondhand trauma in their children. One mother asked me: "My kids can't go to school because their stomachs hurt. Should I make them go, or could something really be wrong?"

Again, I replied that I did not know, but I would find out. And with their help I did. The people of that community taught me about all the faces of loss. And from there, I began to broaden my idea of compassionate crisis care "ministry," expanding it to encompass the whole human "being" in the midst of loss. During the time we spent there, hearing story after story—ten to fifteen hours a day—I became entirely convinced of the impact of loss on every aspect of our beings: physical, emotional, cognitive, and spiritual. Some people were afraid that this would happen again. Some were afraid that they would never recover. Some were afraid they were losing their minds. Some felt guilty because they weren't there to help. Some allowed their emotions to isolate them and feel lonely. Some were angry at the gunman. Some were angry with God. And some were angry with law enforcement officials and medical workers.

The strong resentment I heard in Texas was fueled by the fact that police were involved in a training exercise in a building just next door to the cafeteria. Some of the people were angry at the paramedics because they didn't rush in during the time when no one knew if the gunman was still alive. Logistics didn't matter. People still felt angry at those who they felt could have done something but didn't.

Very soon I noticed that five major emotions were being expressed more than any others—fear, loneliness, guilt, pain, and anger. This community's grief was a process of the entire body, soul, and spirit. So I began to ask my own questions. As a crisis chaplain, I had already made a choice

> He will cover you with his feathers,
> and under his wings
> you will find refuge;
> his faithfulness will be
> your shield and rampart.
>
> *Psalm 91:4*

to take a God's-eye view of my crisis work. I began to ask why we were made this way. What did God have in mind for these obviously normal yet unique responses? He must have a purpose.

And that is what I will share with you in this chapter. As we unlock how your loss affects the "whole" you, we will unfold a better, healthier, more productive way to move through the grieving process that is created in your body for a special purpose. In the previous chapter, we established a working definition of grief. Now let's explore the reality of grief. We'll answer these questions: How does grief affect our bodies? What does grief look like? What does it feel like? What is grief—physically, emotionally, and mentally?

THE PHYSICAL EFFECTS OF GRIEF

Do any of these ailments sound familiar? You can't think straight. You can't eat. You feel angry, depressed, afraid, guilty, and alone.

Then I have good news: You are grieving normally. Let's take these one by one:

Loss of Appetite

One way grief manifests itself is a loss of appetite. In the first few hours of your loss, likely extending for days, you may not have wanted to eat. Your disinterest in food may have continued even as people were constantly shoving it at you with appeals for you to "eat something" to keep up your strength.

> "My life is consumed by anguish and...
> my strength fails."
>
> *Psalm 31:10*

After a funeral, the dinner table is piled high with food that friends, neighbors, and family have brought. And they usually are the only ones eating it all. "Eat, eat," they say to you. And how does that make you feel? It makes you wonder what is wrong. "Something must be wrong if I don't have an appetite." You may begin to feel even more isolated. Depression can also begin to set in.

When I went to Oklahoma City after the bombing at the Murrah Federal Building, I walked into a room full of people waiting around tables to find out whether their loved ones had survived the bombing. You can imagine what the scene looked like. Over four hundred fifty people were milling around a gymnasium set up with table after table, and right down the middle was a buffet line. Tables were stacked with food all down the line. It was the biggest smorgasboard I'd ever seen.

But when I looked around at the individual tables, I saw no food on them at all. I also noticed that nobody was taking food to the tables to eat. Professional psychologists and counselors from all over the world were there to help. Yet it seemed as if no one realized that people who are waiting to hear word of someone they loved would not have an appetite.

When our team joined me, I told them to take cups of water and begin going around the tables and offering them to anyone seated. We began to say to people, "You may not want to eat, and that's okay, but would you drink some water for me?" Before long we had people calling us back to their tables, asking us to sit down with them, to talk and to pray with them. And I would explain to them what I am explaining to you:

It's okay not to be hungry. God allows the body to sustain itself without food for extended periods of time. While you are under stress it's not necessary that you eat, provided you don't have a medical condition, but you do need to keep drinking fluids— juices and water. Avoid coffee, though, or more specifically, caffeine. Caffeine is a dehydrant, and ultimately a depressant. It gives you a lift for a certain amount of time, but you have to keep drinking more caffeine to keep feeling good. So you continue to add to your dehydration. Those who are dealing with the first shock of a loss don't need to be stimulated or dehydrated. So you should limit your intake of coffee as well as soda, since most soft drinks today contain caffeine. Try also to avoid alcohol, since it is ultimately a depressant. Like caffeine, alcohol dehydrates you, plus it lowers your body temperature. It's the last thing that people dealing with grief need. So the idea that you need just a little alcoholic drink to take the edge off can be a dangerous one.

The fact that you don't have an appetite during a crisis is normal. As long as you're drinking water and juices, you'll be fine. And now that you know that, you can be the voice of reason the next time you are helping someone else through a loss.

SELF-CHECK

- No appetite? Remember that your body is made to go without food for extended periods, but not water.

What to do: Drink lots of fluids. Always have a glass or bottle of water in your hand in the days and weeks ahead, whether you feel thirsty or not. If you have a pre-existing medical condition, you should consult a physician immediately.

PAUSE TO REFLECT

Be aware of your diet. What are you eating? Drinking? It *will* affect how you feel. List below what you ate and drank in the last three days:

Breakfast

_____

_____

_____

Lunch

_____

_____

_____

Dinner

_____

_____

_____

Between-meal snacks and drinks, both alcoholic and nonalcoholic

_____

_____

_____

Dehydration, Aches and Pains

You also may be experiencing headaches or body aches—both of which are often a sign of dehydration—as well as stomach problems and digestive problems. You may feel nauseated. Your system is so upset that perhaps you are feeling actual physical pain. Never fear: These are not just phantom pains; they are part of the body's natural way of coping with loss.

Let me explain. When you experience a loss, a dose of adrenalin washes over your system. Your body provides adrenalin to help you deal with the stress—in fact, adrenalin is what causes you to fight or flee. Sometimes we become nauseated as the adrenalin moves through our system. Hence, some people throw up who are not used to large doses of it. Adrenalin also stores in our muscles, thereby causing us great pain. Two natural ways to deal with adrenalin are exercise or hydration.

Again, you need to drink more fluids. You can actually look at yourself and see signs of dehydration. Your skin loses its elasticity. Drink several glasses of water, then check your skin. You'll notice a healthier puffiness that was not there before. Except for the very elderly, the difference is striking—and will help you remember your need for fluids.

Remember, your friends are probably still saying, "Eat, eat!" but they most likely won't know to remind you to drink water, so I will: "Drink, drink!"

SELF-CHECK

- Do you have stomach pains or headaches?

What to do: Drink lots and lots of water for several days. Drink water religiously. Then, check yourself. Have the physical ailments subsided? If not, see a physician.

Fatigue

Do you feel tired to the point of chronic exhaustion? Another physical reaction to loss is fatigue. Remember, you have been—and may still be—under enormous stress. Stress wears us out. Stress can also cause some people's systems to shut down. The neurotransmissions in their brains actually slow down. That's why you can lose the ability to articulate a sentence completely. That's why you can't communicate a whole thought. It's not that you are going crazy, even if that is what you've been thinking. Your brain's chemistry has changed to force you to absorb the loss.

Limit your activity when you feel this way. It's okay to slow down dramatically during this physical change brought on by grief.

Hyperactivity

Some people have just the opposite reaction to the stress of grief. Some may become hyper. They keep going and going and doing and doing, as if on auto-pilot. They have all this excess energy and will work and serve while everyone else gets exhausted and goes to bed. It is almost as if they are trying to exercise their grief away.

These are the "Aunt Marthas" of the world. Like the biblical character Martha, they come and they do everything. They take control. The grieving widow doesn't have to do anything. Aunt Martha is washing, she's cooking, she's cleaning, she's sewing, she's changing the drapes, she's painting the house, she's put new shingles on the roof—she's doing it all. We all have a "Martha" in our family. She may be the widow herself. She won't allow anyone to do anything for her. She won't sit down. She won't let anyone hand her a glass of water; she has to get it herself. She makes all the arrangements. She makes sure everyone who is there to comfort her is comforted and fed. The problem is, nobody recognizes Aunt Martha's grieving. She's the one who calls a counselor two weeks later on the verge of a breakdown. All of a sudden the reality of the loss hits her. Everybody else has gone home, and she's all by herself.

Is this you? If so, you must limit your activity yourself before your body does it for you. Give yourself permission to sit, to let the loss come slowly to you through the "gift" of the grieving process. Allow yourself to be "on hold."

SELF-CHECK

• Are you feeling tired? Are you having a hard time moving from one room to another in your house? Or are you hyper and unable to sit still, even overdoing your exercising or daily tasks?

What to do: Either increase or decrease your activity level in small increments.

Nightmares and Delusions

Experiencing nightmares or even daytime delusions is not abnormal during the grief process. To those experiencing either sensation, though, they're going to feel like they're losing their minds. Sudden dramatic changes in a lifetime of habits can be confusing, especially as your body is going through its own aspects of the grief process.

Consider a new widow who has just lost her husband of forty years. For four decades, she has done things a certain way. She shared her days with him, her routine always including him, even the smallest moments—a cup of morning coffee, an evening meal for two. And now that partner is no longer there. How could she not find herself still seeing and hearing him now and then? I've been married to my wife nineteen years, and I can tell you that if she weren't here tomorrow, I would still feel her presence. There would be times when I would still hear her voice in my house. I would have that sensation of her being around me. I wouldn't be "delusional"; the sensations simply would be part of a normal, natural, transitional grief response because she has been a part of my life for so long.

Another type of delusion or nightmare a grieving person might experience is attempts to change reality. Such a person plays out all the fantasies about the tragedy, especially if it was an accident. They imagine what they would have done if they had been there and how they might have averted the disaster somehow. Then they find themselves in the middle of this nightmare all day, playing it again and again. They go to bed and their body relaxes, but their mind still plays the fantasy on and on.

During my work in New York City after the World Trade Center disaster, I met many people who were in this sort of fixed state, caught in a loop of the tragedy, stuck in a memory. I recall one man in particular who looked dazed, glassy-eyed. "Why did I stay back?" was the first thing he said to me. Soon, I learned his story.

He was a port authority officer who had been working at the World Trade Center on September 11, 2001. On his radio, he could hear fellow officials high in the Twin Towers telling other port authority employees to stay put, that the fire would be contained. Some of their offices were on the highest tower floors. But he was outside seeing the reality of the situation far better than his colleagues inside. Frantically, he began to call into his radio: "No, no! It's not safe! Get out! Get out!" And he continued his warnings until it was too late. Like many firefighters after that morning, he was now living in a strange paradox. He would have rather gone into the buildings to help, even if it meant he would have died. "At least I would have done something," he said.

"But you did do something," I told him. "Had you run in, you wouldn't have been able to understand the scope and the immediate sense of danger the others were in. You'll never know how many people you saved by staying back and sounding the warning."

He looked at me as if he'd never considered this. Yet it was ovious to me—and would have been to anyone else. Finally, with someone who was safe, he was allowing himself to process the facts of the events. He had been trapped in the recurring memory of the September 11 horror. He had experienced the reality of that tragic morning more than a week earlier, but the mind plays self-defense tricks. It often retreats into denial in traumatic times, and the denial can take many forms. A person's "stuck" memory can create scenarios to match the occasion. Sometimes the person is trapped in guilt; other times, in anger or fear or loneliness.

It's not uncommon for victims of tragedies to be unable to access the memory correctly—even though they lived it—until they are able to articulate it. The act of stating the experience out loud allows the person to truly cope with the traumatic event in a healthy way. And those who don't articulate the experience, who stay trapped in the memory, sooner or later will suffer all sorts of harmful reactions—physical, emotional, and spiritual, potentially ranging from nervous breakdowns to drug and alcohol abuse—in order to keep the pain at bay. Healing can only begin when the survivor begins to talk. So in telling his story, the port authority officer was able to begin his personal process of healing.

If you are having nightmares, you also may be one of those people who hasn't expressed your loss well enough, keeping your feelings to yourself. You don't realize that your mind is working like a videotape recorder you cannot turn off. It will keep playing images and memories all day long and into the night because it cannot process it well enough to let it go. The solution is to talk it out. Once you share your "videotape" out loud to a trusted friend or counselor, then your mind will allow the tape to stop running its "sleeping processor" and your waking mind can finish dealing with it. If you don't have someone to share your innermost thoughts with, you can share them via prayer to God. Once you've expressed your "tape," then your mind will hit the stop button on your recorder, and you can move farther along your grief recovery journey.

SELF-CHECK

- Are you having nightmares? Are you seeing things that can't be real during the daytime?

What to do: Don't worry; express your feelings in your journal, and/or find a trusted listener and talk it out.

THE EMOTIONAL EFFECTS OF GRIEF

A few years ago, a San Diego radio station announced a contest offering fifty thousand dollars for anyone who could stay the longest on the city's famous old beach roller coaster. Incredibly, after several weeks, the radio company had to shut down the contest with five people still on the roller coaster who would not, or could not, get off. Reports circulated that one of the remaining riders was going blind, another deaf. And a third person was losing his family. His wife told reporters that she and their kids could not handle it anymore, and if it went on any longer, she might have to leave him.

That situation is a perfect real-life metaphor for the roller coaster ride that the grief process is taking you on. You go up, you come down; you go up, you come down.

Let's look closely at three aspects of this emotional ride.

Feeling Loss of Control

First, your emotions will make you feel out of control. Roller coasters are popular for giving us a taste of this very terrifying feeling. We pay for a cheap thrill, but when the feeling is for real, so is the terror, since most of us work all our lives to be in control of ourselves and our lives.

"I wish I could get hold of the feelings that I'm having." That's the first emotional reaction you may have. Sometimes a person's need for control is so deep that the lack of control creates its own problems. The tragedy's loss is devastating enough, but that you don't have any control over your circumstances anymore can be equally devastating.

If you live in a very ordered world, like I do, then you will feel this effect more than others. I'm what is called a Type-A personality. If you went into my closet, you'd find all the shirts, all the pants, all the jackets, all the sweaters in order. I'm very organized. I live by my daily calendar. Someone like me is going to feel grief's lack of control horribly.

Feeling Nothing at All

Others may experience this loss of control by feeling nothing at all for a while. You may have felt this way—numb, as if in some sort of limbo. You might begin to wonder if you'll ever feel anything again. "Is something wrong with me?" you might say. "I'm not feeling even my grief right now. Aren't I supposed to?"

When my father-in-law passed away, my wife told me of walking out of the house on her way to the airport and wondering why she could still hear the birds sing. Why was life still going on? She had just lost her dad. She had certainly stopped; why hadn't the world?

Remember, whichever response you may be feeling, grieving is unique to each person. Whether you are numb, whether you feel out of control, it is all normal. The ups and downs of the different emotions are confusing as well. And each of the feelings can magnify others. People who are numb often describe a tremendous amount of guilt. They worry that they are not grieving properly, like everybody else seems to be doing. Everyone else is crying, falling apart, while they are being stoic. They're lethargic, almost catatonic, except for a mortified look about them over this sense of grief guilt. "I haven't cried yet," they'll say to me. "I haven't shed any tears yet."

My answer is always: Your tears may come, and they may not. Your grief is unique.

Feeling a Need for Closure

Some people are going to have a great sense of anxiety. Anxiety about not knowing what the future holds: *Where do I go from here? Am I going to get through this? Am I going to be able to cope? Can I get out of bed tomorrow?*

Often, with the loss of life, there is a deep need for physical connection and closure—where is this person that I love so I can go see her?

For closure some people really need to see their loved one who has passed away, and some don't. We must honor both requests.

We need to be careful that we do not rush ourselves. Living in the modern Western culture, we're steadily getting desensitized to death. There is this push just to rush it along. Sometimes that mentality may have its reason and its purpose, but sometimes it doesn't provide the proper closure.

That's why having a memorial service after a death in the family is important. Adults and children alike need it for proper closure. Generations ago, the parlor in the house was the place we would lay the person who died for a viewing. People would come to see the dead friend in the parlor and then gather in the living room to express love and concern for the survivors. We don't make death so personal anymore. We attempt to keep it at arm's-length. That's why the "living room" tradition—the time when friends and family members gather together to support the living and remember the dead—is even more important today than in centuries past. We need the tradition in order not to feel isolated, in order to grieve in a healthy manner.

When you grieve, you are usually going to feel isolated, at least for a time, as if nobody is there for you and nobody understands. But a gathering for a service can ease that isolation for the survivors. The World Trade Center attacks were horrible in many ways, but for the families of the victims, and for the survivors, the fact that most of the bodies would never be recovered stood in the way of proper grieving. The atrocity had created a mass cremation due to the heat of the explosions and the destruction. Normally, even cremations offer something to help the families mourn: ashes. So, in a gesture that spoke poignantly of the communal nature of this massive event—so many dying in one place, so many individuals' ashes coming to rest on the same piece of ground—city officials planned a memorial service for the families. The families would be offered all that was left to offer: cremation containers full of ashes from Ground Zero itself. Perhaps this, city officials decided, would give families who would never have a body to bury something tangible to grieve over, something to acknowledge a death in order to go on with life.

On a Sunday afternoon, victims' families were invited inside Ground Zero to receive an American flag and an urn of ashes. I recall most wrenchingly the reactions of one dead firefighter's young sons: One of the boys grasped the concept, saying it helped him a lot. But the other, younger, son asked, "How do I know this is my dad?" Children have their own special issues, and they express them in unique ways. The city's effort, though, was a vivid acknowledgment of the need to help everyone begin the grief process somehow. The ceremony offered some kind of closure to the grieving families. And since every kind of loss is a death of some kind, then every grief process must entail some sort of closure.

PAUSE TO REFLECT

- If you are feeling anxiety over believing the loss occurred, do you feel you've experienced closure?_____

- What might help you with closure?

_____

_____

Feeling Depression from Emotional Overload

Depression doesn't happen overnight. It comes from a series of emotions that have gotten out of hand. Sometimes all these emotions can get the best of us, and all of a sudden we find ourselves spiraling down and we don't come back up. When those emotions begin to spiral down, big problems can be waiting at the bottom.

If you aren't careful, you can actually become clinically depressed on your roller coaster ride through grief. Clinical depression is a state of being and not an emotion. It will demand treatment. If you find yourself there, please, *please* get help now from a trained professional, especially if you are having suicidal thoughts. People very rarely can work themselves out of their own depression once they get to this point. That's why it is so important that you never pretend the emotions you are feeling don't exist. You may be able to appear fine, but you are not fine on the inside. Health is a whole-body experience during your grief recovery process.

SELF-CHECK

- List some signs of depression.

_____   _____

_____   _____

_____   _____

_____   _____

_____   _____

- Which of these symptoms are you experiencing?

What to do: Talk to your doctor and see if he can help you at this low time in your life.

THE COGNITIVE EFFECTS OF GRIEF

The grief process affects our bodies, our emotions, and our spirits, but also our minds. We mentioned a few of these earlier, and you may have recognized them in your own experience. Have you noticed that you can't think straight? That you often don't finish your sentences? That you can't remember common dates, names, or memories? That you can't think past the loss? That you can't seem to make the simplest decisions? These are the normal effects that grief has on your thought processes.

Difficulty in Making Decisions

This is, perhaps, grief's most common effect on the brain. You will have a hard time making decisions, especially when determining funeral arrangements. For example, you may

SELF-CHECK

Be kind to yourself, but be honest. Write down at least one answer to these questions. Look at them on paper. Do you see it all more logically and calmly? If not, then leave it here, and come back to it tomorrow. Your view may have changed.

• Where are you today on your emotional roller coaster?

_____

• Are you feeling as if no one understands?

_____

• Are you feeling guilty for something you did or didn't do? If so, what is it?

_____

SELF-CHECK

- Are you having trouble making decisions? What is the one decision you are having the most trouble making right now?

_____

What to do: Ask a trusted friend to help you.

struggle to decide between a casket or cremation. Then later, you find that the initial sense of confusion has only eased a little. You become aware that you just aren't quite getting it all together. You might have a thought and then it just slips by or you can't quite grasp it. And time continues to pass while you remain in that state of limbo.

I remember how difficult it was for my mother-in-law to make her first trip to see us after her husband died. My wife and her brother went through a dozen conversations dealing with a dozen flight plans before she could decide on the one she was going to take. She could not make up her mind. My wife at one point wondered, "Is she ever going to get here?" But that is what it's like. Indecisiveness and self-doubt are part of the cognitive effect that grief has on your thinking process.

I suggest strongly that you not make any long-term decisions for a while after a loss—especially moving. A lot of people suddenly decide to move away. Unconsciously, the idea is, no doubt, an effort to find relief: "If I can just get out of this scene, my troubles won't follow me." But that is unwise. A move made too quickly may mean losing all your support system you've had for years and years. Such a move could make you really isolated.

Try not to make any long-term decisions within the first year after the loss. It's not the time to sell your house and the family business and move away. If you can hold out financially and emotionally and physically for a year, you will have more clarity in your thinking and be farther along in your grief process.

SELF-CHECK

• Are you contemplating a big decision today? How long has it been since your loss?

What to do: Consider what would happen if you waited a little while before making it. Anything negative? If not, wait and see if you feel the same way later.

Inability to Articulate Thoughts

Along with the slowed-down thinking that is part of being unable to make decisions, you may also find yourself, at times, starting a sentence and not completing it. I notice that when I am invited to eat with a person going through the grief process, I have to slow down. I'll be done with lunch and they'll be on the first bite. It's a struggle for them to even collect their thoughts. "I can't remember what I was just going to say," is something I hear quite a bit during such encounters.

It's always a little embarrassing for the grieving person, so I strive to be a good listener. That's what you need right now—good listeners. The most important thing I will say is what I'm saying to you now: You may imagine you will always feel this way, but you won't. It's natural. It's normal. And it's only temporary when you keep moving through your grief recovery in a healthy manner.

Memory Lapses and Repetition

You may have problems with such simple mental functions as recall also. Memory lapses and repetition are a common effect of the grief process. I always suggest that a person going through grief because of a death in the family take someone with them to the funeral home. You will be surprised what a hard time you have with just the basic information. What was your husband's middle name? Where was he born? You celebrated his birthday for forty years and suddenly you can't remember it. And those are the easy questions. Choosing caskets or planning services demands an even greater level of cognitive interaction. The funeral director is waiting for your answers, but you can't be sure they are the right ones. A trusted friend or family member might be responsible for bringing the birth certificate and helping fill out forms. Remember, the funeral director has just met you and may not understand all of your concerns. I know because I have been asked to conduct corporate training for mortuaries, sensitizing their employees to what they will face daily—other people's death and grief.

Also, don't be surprised if you find out that you are repeating things. Grieving people commonly do this. When I work with people in crisis, I notice that they often need to tell me the same story the next day and the next day and the next. They may have forgotten that they told me the story, or they are struggling to turn off their mental video-tape recorders and finally process some important things. Sometimes the story isn't necessarily something related to the loss, but a significant memory of some kind about the loved one they've lost or from whom they're separated. Maybe the memory is reliving certain good times. In my training sessions, I teach how to be a "dedicated listener" for just such situations—how to be patient while each person wades through his or her unique grief process. You'll find some guidance in listening in Appendix 2 of this book.

Flashbacks and Fixations

If you're not careful, you can become fixated on the loss or continue to have flashbacks of certain events related to your crisis. I have had people tell me a story, tears streaming down their face, as if it happened yesterday. I ask, "When did this happen?" Too often, the answer is years before: five years, ten years, even twenty years ago. This is natural and normal as you move through the grief process. The concern comes when the fixations last, when you are still talking emotionally about a crisis years later. That can be a sign of unchecked, chronic grief.

God allows the mind to slow down and function on a basic needs level—to assimilate the magnitude of a loss and bring about the appropriate resources for recovery. Our bodies are wonderfully and uniquely made. If you had to comprehend and function in your full faculties and absorb the full loss immediately, you would literally self-destruct. Your mind couldn't handle it. But God so wisely created our bodies in a way that we are forced to slow down and process the loss while we look for the help we need. That, of course, makes finding the help we need crucial.

Let's discuss the dangers of stopping or detouring the grief process before it has time to do its God-designed function.

SIGNS OF "CHRONIC" GRIEF

When grief is not processed in a healthy way, it becomes what is called "chronic grief."

Behavioral Signs of Chronic Grief

If you don't recognize your grief and deal with it properly, you can count on behavioral changes appearing. Some behaviors that are signs that you may not be dealing properly with your grief include:

Self-medication. When grief turns chronic, you can actually start having things go wrong physically. Your body starts breaking down and you may start compensating for the breakdown through self-medication, through destructive relationships, through alcohol or drug abuse. You will find something that will take the pain away.

Over-indulgence in positive behaviors. Some people's chronic grief behavior will include actions that are normally very good. Believe it or not, some chronic grievers become super-spiritual. Anytime the church doors are open they are there, working hard to hide an

SELF-CHECK

- Are you continuing to feel out of control? Remember that your body affects your mind. There may be a physical cause for the cognitive effect.

What to do: Avoid artificial stimulants as much as possible.

unfinished grief process. I think of one case in particular: A woman in one church, a mother of five young children, lost her husband. On Monday night, she came to the singles class at the church. On Tuesday night, she attended the grief class. She faithfully attended the midweek service, and on Thursday, a special support group. Friday night was a home fellowship circle, and she went to that. Saturday offered a corporate prayer group, and Sunday she went to church services. Does that sound like positive behavior for a young widowed mother? Before you answer, let me say that the children spent all their time in the nursery. In essence, the children lost both parents.

Men most often will overwork. They think, *I'll just work through my grief; that will solve it. After all, I had to take four days off, and I lost that pay. And the funeral will cost some money so I've got to work overtime.* We all need to be careful about over-indulging any behavior.

Physical Signs of Chronic Grief

Physical signs that indicate you may not be dealing well with your grief include:

Sleeplessness that persists long after the event. At first it's normal to have sleepless nights. But if six months to a year later you're still not sleeping, then you need to revisit your grief. You need to ask yourself, "Am I allowing God to walk me through the grief process? If not, why not?"

Frequent episodes of hearing and seeing things that are not there. Initially, you may have a sense of seeing your loved one or hearing his voice, but you will soon adjust to reality.

When such episodes, or physical manifestations as they are called, don't diminish after several months, it is clear that people are not dealing with their grief. They are looking for an answer not based in reality, because reality hurts far too much.

Frequent episodes of confusion or bewilderment that become detrimental to your welfare. If you continue to feel confused and bewildered as the weeks and months go by, you have probably made the mistake of thinking that it will all go away by itself. Such sensations could also be products of too much continued medication. You can actually wonder why you are so sleepy as you still take those tranquilizers prescribed to help you through the first hours of your tragedy. Most mental health drugs are meant as temporary aids, allowing you time to access other resources that will assist you in your journey. My fear is that we sometimes overmedicate ourselves instead of allowing our natural grief process to work. Take clues from your body; it will tell you a clear story about how you are processing your grief.

Emotional Signs of Chronic Grief

Emotional signs that indicate you may not be dealing well with your grief include:

Isolation—physical and emotional withdrawal. The withdrawal of energy from previously healthy relationships is the last danger sign of not dealing with our grief. "Nobody understands," you might tell yourself, "so I have to do this all on my own." Emotionally you withdraw, building walls around yourself. You never go out to dinner with any of your friends anymore, you don't go to parties, and you don't laugh.

I spend a lot of time during my compassionate crisis care training sessions teaching others to recognize isolation because it is such a big danger sign. Isolation is a natural tendency for a grieving person. It's the way we protect ourselves from being hurt. So I train others to notice the signs and to reach out and draw out those going through the grief process so they don't feel like they are alone. I teach that no one can feel the grief for survivors, but anyone can certainly be a shoulder to cry on, an arm to lean on, and an ear to listen.

> The LORD is compassionate and gracious, slow to anger, abounding in love.
>
> *Psalm 103:8*

The power of presence is so strong that you don't have to have answers. Two good ears are great tools that God has given us to help a person avoid the danger of grief withdrawal. If you begin to notice that you are cutting yourself off from friends and from life, call someone. Gradually work your way back into the relationships of those who care for you. And be assured that, even if you need some time away from people, you are never alone. God is always with you.

EFFECTS OF CHRONIC GRIEF

Chronic grief can come at any time from any loss. And we must recognize it as quickly as possible. If you aren't permitted to grieve, no matter what the loss—be it large or small

SELF-CHECK

- How has your faith helped you in your grief this week?

_____

- How have you allowed your family or friends to reach out to you recently? How did it make you feel?

_____

in the eyes of the world—you'll develop chronic grief. You'll get stuck in the process and never move forward. The result will make you alive physically, but quite possibly dead emotionally and spiritually.

Chaplaincies, as part of police and fire services, have grown in the last fifteen years due to the recognition of this dynamic. A loved one's traumatic death can cause psychological damage that could play out devastatingly, sometimes months and years in the future. How often do we hear about an elderly person dying and the spouse passing quickly thereafter? In Oklahoma City's federal building bombing, 168 people died. Since then, six people—both survivors and victims' loved ones—have committed suicide. Statistically, the number of suicides-in-waiting from the World Trade Center disaster's almost three thousand deaths is heart-stopping. And yet your loss can be just as dangerous if you aren't careful about your own grief process.

Your faith can help your grief recovery. Remember, your grief process has been created by God for a purpose. He gives us emotions during the grief process as warning signs to show us where our needs are. And your healthy grief recovery efforts all begin with acknowledging those needs.

Work It Out

Do you see yourself in any of the descriptions of chronic grief? Relax and know that you are normal. Make a date with yourself to check what you wrote down in one month's time to see if you are still experiencing the same thing. But for now, answer the questions below:

1. What one thing bothers you the most right now?

_____

_____

_____

_____

2. What grief tendencies are you displaying?

_____

_____

_____

_____

3. From what you've learned, what can you do to help yourself prevent or overcome your grief?

_____

_____

_____

4. Compare symptoms with your loved ones. If others have experienced the same loss, how are you all responding differently? What are the similarities? How are you giving one another permission to grieve uniquely and individually with this loss?

_____

_____

_____

5. Don't fight your emotions; learn to acknowledge them. In this space, begin to use God's resource, the Bible, to help you accept how you feel. Read Psalm 77:1-20. Summarize it below in your own words, for your own situation:

_____

_____

_____

6. Look for people around you who can help bring balance to your emotional roller coaster existence right now by listening to your thoughts. Name two of those people:

_____

_____

THE EMOTIONS OF LOSS

Now it's time to apply all the basics you've learned thus far and tackle your specific issues head on. Which strong emotion is keeping you from pressing on? Which one do you need to push out of the way before it trips you?

You'll recall that in my experience of hearing thousands of stories from people in crisis, I have recognized five areas of strong emotion that most people will find to be a problem in grief recovery: fear, loneliness, guilt, pain, and anger.

People often say, "I want my emotions under control. I can't do anything until they are." But there may be a reason they are coming at you so strongly. We know the negative effects of the five emotions, but God made them, so there must be a good side as well. Before we plunge headlong into the chapters to come, consider this question: *What are the emotions I'm feeling right now telling me? Where are the flashing lights turning my focus— and why?* Here is a possibility for each:

- *Fear* can teach us boundaries.
- *Loneliness* can help us recognize our need for relationship with God.
- *Guilt* can draw us to acknowledge our failures.
- *Pain,* in the sense of suffering, can help us grow in character.
- *Anger* can help us draw the line of right and wrong.

Do you agree? In the next five chapters, with the help of your new tools, we'll discover these emotions as they were meant to be used during the God-given grieving process.

Grief Recovery Journal

Date _____

Dear _____ :

This is how I feel right now:

_____

_____

_____

_____

_____

_____

_____

_____

_____

_____

_____

This is what I've discovered today:

_____

_____

_____

_____

_____

_____

_____

_____

_____

_____

This is what I still question today:

_____

_____

_____

_____

_____

_____

_____

_____

_____

_____

Extra space to finish your thoughts, if needed:

_____

_____

_____

_____

_____

_____

_____

_____

_____

For additional encouragement, listen to Number 6 on the *Grief Recovery Workbook CD*

Chapter 6

Fear:
Why Am I So Afraid?

Joyce Dail was my first secretary. She was one of those faithful and supportive Christian women who would do anything for anyone. A mother of two grown boys and a girl herself, she was so trustworthy that we asked her to baby-sit our first child when my wife returned to work. Just like the rest of us, she had her own struggles and pain. But she lived a godly life, and we were blessed to have her in our lives. Then one day she was diagnosed with cervical cancer. For the next few years she fought a gallant fight, and as she did, she taught me how not to be afraid.

It's normal to fear the worst that life can throw at us. Yet when the worst does happen, some people go through it with great faith. That was Joyce. When she was first diagnosed, the doctors initially gave her only a short time to live. But she chose to fight that prognosis. This is a woman who had surgeries and rounds of chemotherapy, and even suffered through an experience called stem cell washing, a procedure in which all of her blood was drained out of her system, washed, and put back in. That fight forced her to lie in an isolated room for months in order to avoid infections.

Yet despite her harsh treatments, Joyce traveled the United States with her husband. They traveled almost six thousand miles visiting all the places she had ever wanted to see and doing all the things she had ever wanted to do. I think she set a record for visiting the most malls in America!

This was a woman who took her wig off and said it was okay, a woman who embraced life, even on her bad days. She had to grieve the loss of her life every day she had left on this earth. Yet she taught us that even though we'll all die, we don't have to live in fear. "Whether I live or die I'm going to be okay," she told me. "I'd love to live. I want to be here. I want to watch my grandkids grow up. But I don't control that. I only control how I face it." We were there at the end, and she slipped into eternity with great peace. Yet Joyce is with me every day in some ways, her life a testament to the ability not only to control fear but to triumph over it. She continues to profoundly affect me and the way I have viewed my work with others in crisis during all the years since.

FEAR IS A NORMAL RESPONSE

> Trust in the LORD forever, for the LORD, the LORD, is the Rock eternal.
>
> *Isaiah 26:4*

What scares you the most about your loss? Just asking that question is a fearful thing because we have to admit that we've had a loss, coming face to face with the reality of it. Sometimes we don't even know we're afraid.

We have the "gift" of fear for a purpose. It draws safe boundaries for us. It shows us the harmful areas of our life. It's good, for example, that our parents showed us that the stove is hot. That's a healthy fear. It's wise that we teach our children to be afraid to cross the street without looking both ways. In my house, before we let our children "surf" the Internet, we put stopgaps in place that will protect them from getting into the unhealthy areas. Our fear for what our children may experience before they are mature is a very healthy, practical, helpful parenting tool.

Modern culture says we shouldn't be afraid of anything. But that isn't exactly true. We should be cautious and wary as we live life. Doing so teaches us to be afraid of the things that can harm us.

There is the fear that causes us to be wary of danger from surprise. This is the kind that can be dangerous for others as well as yourself. That's certainly true in our house. When we were first married, my wife used to like to scare me. Before I was a crisis chaplain, I was in law enforcement. I've been trained in self-defense techniques, so I'm not the kind of guy you want to scare. I'm likely to drop-kick you into tomorrow. Literally. That's the reason police officers have to be very careful when they are off duty. One time my wife thought it would be fun to surprise me by jumping out at me from a dark part of our house. Before I knew it, I had her pinned on the carpet. I thought it was someone who had broken into the house. I didn't have to think about it. I just responded.

And then there is fear that lingers. This kind of fear can really grip our lives, especially when it begins early in a child's mind. I almost didn't attend college because of fear. When I was a little boy living in Brooklyn, New York, I heard that a young student at New York University was killed on the campus, and I remember actually articulating this thought: "I'm not ever going to college because college is a dangerous place and you could be killed." That stuck and set into motion a deep dread of the idea of attending a university of any kind. From there I somehow went on to conclude that I was not college material.

When I graduated from twelfth grade and announced that I didn't want to go to college, my father was upset—he thought I was being lazy and apathetic. And he forced me, literally, past my fear. He dragged me down to the university, introduced me to a guidance counselor, and admitted me into the university in the way you would admit a person to a hospital.

Thank God he helped me with that! It wasn't that I was apathetic. I had allowed a childhood fear to grow into two serious young adult fears—the illogical fear that anybody who went to the university would likely be killed, and the ensuing fear of my own incompetence, a fear that I wouldn't be able to compete at that level. Both fears were shortly proven wrong, of course. Had I never gone to college, I would never have become a crisis chaplain, and I would never, ever have become the kind of person who could be talking to you through the words of this workbook.

So fear can have a devastating impact in our lives if we let it rule us—whatever its source. It is an emotion that we feel for a lot of different reasons, but our focus for the rest of this chapter will be on the kind that comes from a loss. Let's look back at the definition of *grief:* "Grief is the normal process of natural emotions and feelings which are uniquely experienced after any loss of any relationship."

During grief from traumatic events, it's normal that you feel a sense of fear, of apprehension. We think when we stuff our emotions that we've dealt with our fear, but we've simply developed an unhealthy habit. Remember, a nonresponse is a response. You find yourself unconsciously secluding yourself out of fear of what might happen—I don't go out at night, or I don't let down my guard, or I don't join that group. In all those don'ts there is a response. Being in the grip of an almost unconscious fear habit can control an entire portion of your daily life.

TYPICAL GRIEF PROCESS FEARS

Let's examine some of the fears that a loss may produce that can stunt the grief process. You may recognize some of the following in your own experience:

Fear of the Loss Reoccurring

You may be afraid that the pain of the loss could happen again. You might be afraid to enter into new relationships for fear you may have to grieve again. You build up a "fear wall" that keeps you away from both good and bad in the big world out there.

Fear of Where the Loved One Has Gone

Even in Christian circles, a crisis brings on a need for specifics. The questions I hear often after a loss by death are: "Where is my loved one?" "What has happened to my loved one?" "What's it like there?" The uncertainty is overwhelming in a grieving state of mind, especially after miscarriages, infant deaths, or childhood deaths.

Fear of Being Unable to Care for Yourself

"Am I going crazy?" As you may recall from chapter 5, grief affects the body and mind. There can be a lingering fear of the seemingly mental imbalance that comes with a tragic shock. "Will I not be able to think straight again? Will I be able to have a normal life again?"

Fear of Financial Insecurity

This is the fear of not being able to care for yourself financially, if you were not the bread-winner of the family. In today's world, where two-income families are often needed to make ends meet, even a divorce can cause this sort of fear. But if you are a widow who has found great fulfillment in taking care of your spouse who "brought home the bacon," you may have real financial fears after he has died.

The Fear of Living Alone

"Am I going to be alone for the rest of my life?" "Is this going to be my life forever, being all by myself?" A tremendous amount of fear can come from the thought of being alone, and if this is your fear, you are not alone in feeling it.

The Fear of Rejection

"My spouse has rejected me, so is everybody going to reject me?" Perhaps that's your fear. Or maybe the death of your spouse or your only child makes you feel as if you won't be needed anymore. "What is my sense of purpose? God, am I still significant?"

Fear of the Professionals Involved in Your Loss

You may find yourself avoiding police, doctors, or even ministers, depending on how your loss happened and what kind of relationship you had with those who took care of your loved one or performed any type of service during your crisis. Maybe one of these people said something inappropriate, or maybe their very presence is such a reminder of your loss that you dodge them.

Did you recognize yourself in any of those fears that easily come during the grief process? Some fears will be obvious, some will take a little longer to grasp. And you may easily have several fears lurking in the dark areas of your grief recovery process. Now is the time to name them and then conquer them. Let's try to answer these three questions about your fears:

- Fear of whom?
- Fear of what?
- What's the reason for my fear?

The world's philosophy is *Get on, get up, and get over. Get on with life.*

Not me. Sometimes when I walk down the path early in the morning or late at night, I hear rustling in the bushes and trees. Initially my heart rate increases, I sweat more, and my sense of awareness is heightened. At this point I have a choice: run and hide, or stay on the path and face my fear. Let's take a step toward understanding your fear, giving yourself a bit of mercy, and giving God a chance to help you move on.

IDENTIFYING THE FEAR

How can we get rid of something if we're not sure what it is? First we have to identify our fears before we can overcome them.

Face the Fear

I have learned that when the bushes rustle, there is something to be discovered. Rather than running, I now search until I find the source! Running away can be your biggest stumbling block to continuing down the road to recovery. Why? It's hard to let God into the process when you can't bring yourself to face the source of the fear. For some people the problem is not that they don't have a desire to pray, and it's not that they don't have a desire to use God's scriptural resources. The obstacle is that they are afraid of God's anger over their conflicted spiritual feelings. Their whole theology is mixed up with lightning bolts and wrath. But that's not God. Everything we believe and everything we know as Christians says that he loves to share the secrets of the universe with us through his Word. So if your fear is God's anger, you never will go to him with your pain until you acknowledge these feelings of fear. In other words, try looking under the bushes—there *is* something to discover.

It's like physical therapy, isn't it? Physical therapy has to be the worst part of the injury. I once broke my little finger. The surgery was nothing. The therapy, however, was

SELF-CHECK

Search your heart and think about your fears.

As you begin to know the answers, turn back to this page and make notes to yourself. Seeing them on the page will help loosen their grip on you.

- Fear of whom?

- Fear of what?

- What's the reason for your fear?

---

torture, having to bend the finger after it had been stiff so long. At one point I said, "Hey, just cut the finger off! That suits me better than this pain."

Facing the fear is our physical therapy; it's painful but necessary. We need the rehab to complete the work that God has started in us with the healing of our grief. Nothing is impossible with God; the Lord said he will be faithful to complete what he's started. We just have to allow it.

I'll make a deal with you. I will tell you my most basic fear, if you'll tell me yours.

I was abandoned when I was ten months old. It's a miracle not only that I'm alive, but that I'm healthy, and mentally and spiritually stable. However, I wasn't the husband I really could have been to my wife. I was afraid of her.

Having been raised in a home where my father was an alcoholic and where my mother went out for bread one day and didn't come back, I had a lot of fears. Then when I began working in law enforcement, I saw the worst of humanity on a daily basis, especially in family relationships. So my major fear in my marriage relationship was that I was always going to be rejected by my wife. Yes, she loved me now, but it wouldn't last. Once she really found out my faults she wouldn't stay.

Then, when my daughter Kimberlee was born, I had all kinds of crazy fears. Would I crush her if I held her? Would I lose my temper and hurt her by shaking her or spanking her too hard? I had seen enough of those types of incidents in my work to give cause for worry. And if I wasn't even capable of being a good father, wouldn't my wife think less of me? All of these fears began to grow over the course of those early years in my marriage. Rather than ruin my marriage, I really had to come to grips with my fears about my relationship with my wife and my child. What saved my marriage was that I faced those fears.

I found that my fear wasn't unfounded, just misdirected. My wife might indeed reject me and leave me. The possibility, however small, is still real. Yet I don't need to be a controller or a manipulator in my relationship with her to feel "safe." And the reason for that freedom is that I serve a God who will never leave me and never reject me. No one can take me away. How did I come to this conclusion? I was able to face my fears by using one of the tools you now have. I used the resource of resources—the Bible. The answers I found there told me what God had to say on the matter. He'd say, "Ray, you are accepted by me. You're secure in me, and I have a plan and a purpose for your life."

To bring that feeling of fear full circle back to the One who created the emotion of fear is to bring us into the revelation of God's Word. God's truth helps us to process our fears so we can walk in the freedom that the gospel has provided for us. It takes us to another level of seeing—a new perspective. And that new perspective allows us to face our fears.

So I can ask myself: Why am I afraid?

What about you? Why are *you* afraid? Can the source of your fear be something in your past? Is it present circumstances or unresolved past conflicts? You might be surprised to find out that the fear really may be coming from another source and has been revived by all the emotions you're feeling in the grief of your loss. It may be from an old hurt that never healed or an old fear never faced.

Use Prayer

I used to walk and pray in a community I was ministering in. Every day I would walk past the homes and pray for the people inside. As I made my way past a chain-link fence one winter morning, I was greeted by a large Rottweiler dog. Fortunately, he was inside the fence. At this point I had a choice: run from my fear and never return again, or face my fear and continue to pray.

Not knowing the dog's name, I called him "Jesus." "Jesus, Jesus, Jesus," I would call out as I passed that home each day! It was my way of praying through my fear.

> "As a mother comforts her child, so will I comfort you."
> *Isaiah 66:13*

What is the purpose of prayer in your strategy to overcome your fears surrounding your loss? Prayer is God's gift to you. It's your package from him, your line of communication with him. He gave us prayer as a tool to help us share our fears, our anger, our anxiety, as well as our happiness and joy. Prayer gives us a place to acknowledge our concerns to Somebody who will be able to handle them, who won't tell them to anybody else. If you don't ever open the gift of prayer, you will never know the joy of being in communication with God.

SELF-CHECK

- What is the source of your fear? Is it a current situation, or is it unresolved past conflicts?

_____

- Is it your present situation, or something in your past that can't let you see it all clearly?

_____

- Name one thing from your background that might be fueling your fears.

_____

Confide in a Trusted Friend

You might need a friend to help you process the source of your fears. Looking back through my own life and questions, the greatest lessons I've learned have come from people in my life who have been mentors to me. They say to me, "Hey, let's deal with this."

Friends help us analyze whether our fears are legitimate. All of our fears are real to us, but a friend can help validate or legitimize them—or deflate them. Is it a healthy fear or an unhealthy fear? Friends can also help us identify the source of fear. So seek out a trusted friend. Tell him or her your fear, and some thoughts about its source, then listen closely. You're the one who can finally decide whether what you hear is true, which makes asking for God's participation in your choice of the friend even more important.

FREEING YOURSELF FROM FEAR

How do we become free of our fears? Here are some of the ways I have found that work for those in grief recovery:

Uncover and Face the Source of the Fear

Using the resources from chapter 3, the help of your trusted friend, and insight from prayer, uncover the source of your fear, then be open and honest about it—first with yourself, then with God. Tell God how you feel. He already knows how you feel anyway. If we can't be clean before God, our heavenly Father, the one who created us and has loved us more than anybody could ever love us, how can we be open and honest with anybody else?

> This is what the LORD says—"Fear not, for I have redeemed you; I have summoned you by name; you are mine."
>
> *Isaiah 43:1*

Use the Bible, the resource God gave us. Notice the thought in Isaiah 43:1. What a beautiful promise to remember! You are his. You may be going through a terrible separation or divorce. You may have lost the most important person in your life and feel

SELF-CHECK

❧

- You need a trusted helper, a friend, a mentor—someone who knows you and your situation. Who might that be? And why?

_____

_____

_____

SELF-CHECK

- Look up the following scriptures and summarize below the one that speaks to you the loudest:

Isaiah 66:13   Psalm 4:8   Isaiah 26:3-4

_____

_____

_____

all alone. The Lord reminds you through Scripture that you are his. You can claim that promise from his Word, but you have to know it first. The only way that this resource will have any positive effect on your fear is to use the Bible as it was intended: Know the promises it offers. We won't walk in freedom of fear if we don't believe what God's Word says about us.

Face the Fear Slowly

Fear of water is a perfect illustration of this idea. Let's say you fear the water. Why do you fear it? Perhaps it's because you've never learned how to swim. Perhaps it's more traumatic, and you actually saw someone drown or nearly drown. One time, I was with a

> I will lie down and
> sleep in peace,
> for you alone, O LORD,
> make me dwell in safety.
>
> *Psalm 4:8*

bunch of kids at a pool and I just assumed they could all swim. Suddenly one of the kids jumped in and grabbed me. "Wow, could you play a little less rough?" I said. Then I realized he didn't know how to swim. I saw the fear in his eyes. He was going to drown, and he was going to drown me too. That kind of fear can keep you from ever coping with your problem.

What are some ways you could get over being afraid to go in the water? You might take a classroom course on swimming, getting all the facts first. But you can't put that swimming manual under your pillow at night and hope to wake up knowing how to swim. You never really learn anything until you do it. So you ease into the water and begin practicing a few strokes. Then, finally, you put your head in. You immerse yourself. It's that way for swimming; it's that way for any of your other fears. Before you know it, you're swimming. And the more you swim, the bet-

> For God has not given us a spirit of fear, but of power and love and of a sound mind.
>
> *2 Timothy 1:7* (NKJV)

ter swimming muscles you develop. The more you exercise your faith, the bigger your spiritual muscles become. Soon you can find yourself saying, "Wow! What was I afraid of? God had the answer the whole time."

Don't Give Up

This isn't a one-day dynamic. You won't wake up tomorrow and not be afraid anymore. There are many steps along the journey. You don't learn to swim with one lesson; you don't become unafraid in one day. It takes practice; it takes time. Be patient. Don't try just once and give up.

Be sensitive and patient with yourself. And watch closely: God may want to teach you more than just how to overcome a fear. God may want to stretch you beyond what you think you are even capable of. He may plan to take you to a whole new depth. Remember, God will do his part, but we must do ours.

As you have hidden his Word in your heart, as it becomes a lifeline to you and holds you and surrounds you and keeps you afloat, you can slowly watch the fear factor of your grief recovery subside.

Work It Out

1. Can you articulate your worst fear?

_____

_____

_____

_____

2. Why do you think this fear is haunting you most?

_____

_____

_____

3. What are some safe environments in which you can face your fears?

_____

_____

_____

_____

4. From what you've learned in this chapter, how might you prepare for the fears you will face in your grief recovery?

_____

_____

_____

Grief Recovery Journal

Date _____

Dear _____ :

This is how I feel right now:

_____

_____

_____

_____

_____

_____

_____

_____

_____

_____

_____

_____

This is what I've discovered today:

_____

_____

_____

_____

_____

_____

_____

_____

_____

_____

This is what I still question today:

_____

_____

_____

_____

_____

_____

_____

_____

_____

_____

Extra space to finish your thoughts, if needed:

_____

_____

_____

_____

_____

_____

_____

_____

_____

_____

For additional encouragement, listen to
Number 7 on the *Grief Recovery Workbook CD*

Chapter 7

Loneliness:
Why Do I Feel So Alone?

In 1990, a Vietnam veteran in the middle of a flashback sat across the street from an elementary school in Stockton, California—a school heavily attended by Southeast Asian children—and began to shoot them as they played on the school grounds. He killed over half a dozen children before he turned the gun on himself.

The children's families were remarkably alone in their grief, and professional efforts at helping them were almost useless. First, there was a language barrier. Most of the family members didn't speak English. The cultural barrier, however, was more than just a barrier; it was an all-but-impenetrable wall between themselves and their grief. Part of the Southeast Asian belief system included the teaching that if a family member wept for a dead child, the child's spirit would forever be trapped, hindered from going on to the next life by the loved ones. And that belief, in essence, also trapped the family members in their loneliness. That was their own unique grief process, their own journey they had to travel alone.

But the real story I want to share is about Gene, an Anglo-American teacher at the school who truly wrestled with and then overcame loneliness. Immediately after the crisis, he found it almost impossible to return to work. His Christian faith was deep, but while it gave him a foundation, he still struggled, primarily because of how very alone he felt. First, his loneliness was fueled by guilt. He had not been able to stop the horror he saw on this most innocent of American places, a schoolyard. Second, he also was a Vietnam veteran, so he found himself feeling deep empathy for not only the Southeast Asian families but also for the gunman. Third, he couldn't communicate his feelings to the families, of the children he taught because of their own unique grief process. He was slipping. "Should I quit my job?" he wondered. "What am I going to do?" How was he going to get past the incredible loneliness of his grief?

Gene was one of the primary people I came to know during that crisis. He got past his loneliness in two ways. He found an internal way and an external way to help him find and stay on his road to recovery from his horrendous loss. He would express his grief through writing poetry, and he would reach out to the others who were hurting in the community. He became instrumental in bringing We Care, our compassionate crisis care ministry, to train him and his fellow church members how to reach out. One of the first Healing the Broken Heart seminars we conducted in a large setting happened because Gene worked to find a way past the roadblock of his own loneliness.

It's one thing to choose to be alone. Almost daily I sneak away to be alone on purpose so I can pray. I'll turn off the pager and lose the cell phone and not tell anyone where I'm going. This is the type of aloneness that is good for one's soul.

It's another thing to be in the middle of a crowd and feel alone. You can be married, you can be surrounded by your children, you can be in an assembly of people and feel lonely. You can be in freeway traffic or in a crowded stadium and feel like there is no one else who knows what you are going through.

This is the aloneness that produces loneliness, and it is anything but good for one's soul. It's also another normal emotion that you'll experience during your grief process. This kind of loneliness can come over you like a sudden tide.

Well-known Christian writer Elisabeth Elliot is a woman who knows loneliness. She once wrote, "Loneliness is one of those terms of our humanness." To be human is to feel lonely. It's inescapable.

How does Elisabeth know? In the 1950s, her husband, Jim Elliot, and four other missionaries were massacred while attempting to make contact with an Ecuadorian tribe. Most people know her in the context of this event. But Elisabeth married again. And in that relationship, she had the painful task of watching her second husband die as well, this time through cancer.

She wrote another quote in her book *The Path of Loneliness* that has stayed with me: "Events do not change souls. It is our response to those events which finally affect us." Elisabeth Elliot has been where you are—twice. And she declares that how we respond to a tragic event, not the event itself, is what can and should dictate our lives.

In this chapter, we are going to look at your loneliness from the following three angles in hopes of helping you apply the same kind of hard-earned wisdom to this aspect of your grieving process: the cycle of loneliness, the surprise of loneliness, and strategies for loneliness.

THE CYCLE OF LONELINESS

There are two ways a person coping with grief will respond to loneliness. Your symptoms will fall into two categories—moving toward people and withdrawing from people. As we talk about these, see which applies to your own life:

Moving Toward People

The first attempt to overcome your loneliness will be a physical one. Some people join every group in sight. They work at being around other people at all times, because they think that's what is going to solve their loneliness. They say, "If I meet new people or go someplace, I won't feel lonely."

A very interesting cultural phenomenon has developed over the last few years because of the innate loneliness of being human: chat rooms on the Internet. Think about this concept. You are alone at your computer, and you are typing out a conversation to people whom you've never met in person. It is rather like a detached confessional of sorts. It's a novel way not to be lonely while being alone.

When typing on a screen doesn't fill the void, strangers over the telephone have become an option. There are "900" calls in which you pay to talk to a stranger on the other end, be it a psychic, a dating service, or even a fan club. These "services" have become extremely lucrative scams because of the sea of loneliness the human condition creates. And humans seem to be willing to pay anything for it. I have seen monthly bills exceeding $1,600 for people who have just wanted conversation. Something momentarily is nurtured in those conversations; we don't feel as alone, and our imaginations fill in the rest. And who needs fantasy more than a person who has just received an overdose of reality through a painful loss?

Yet we are still alone.

Moving Away from People

The other way to overcome your loneliness is a 180-degree turn—you avoid people. You become skeptical of other people's motives. You may say, "Nobody understands me." "What is their motive for befriending me?" "They don't really want to be my friend; they want something from me."

That seems almost a paradox, doesn't it? A lonely person can isolate on purpose, automatically withdrawing from other people. You can easily feel this way while working through the grief process. A mother who has lost a child doesn't want to be around other mothers and small children. She may not even be able to be around other people at all, because they will be laughing and enjoying themselves, and she still feels totally unable to laugh again. She may not be alone in the sense of isolation—she may have a husband and other children—but she feels all alone. "How are you?" her friends ask her. She answers: "Fine." And normal chitchat follows as she sinks back into her loneliness. As that pattern continues, she can become bitter, starting to resent everyone around her because no one is pulling her out of her loneliness. She doesn't even notice that she is the one pulling away. And after a while, her friends will stop trying to reach out to her.

Like that mother, we can feel alone in our grief, isolate ourselves, and then become bitter when others seem to move away from us. When that happens, we build a wall of sympathy and pity that becomes an identity. It's a devastating cycle that you can stop only if you catch it early. And that comes from being aware of the danger. The alternative is a slow slide into a chronic grief situation that you'll find very hard to break.

In my experience in hundreds of crisis situations with hundreds of grieving people, I have found one sure-fire way to break the mourner's unhealthy loneliness cycle: I never ask, "How are you doing?" Instead, I listen and observe, and then comment on what I see.

SELF-CHECK

- You are in a crowd. A stranger asks you, "How are you?"

How do you answer?_____

- Now, a trusted, nonjudgmental, knowing friend walks up, touches your arm, looks you straight in your eyes, and says, "Tell me how you *really* are."

How might you answer?

_____

_____

_____

Do I have to ask the widow how she is when I arrive at her home at 2 o'clock in the afternoon and she is still in her robe and pajamas? When I gently comment on what I'm observing—saying to the widow, for example, "I see it has been a hard night and a long morning. Please tell me about it"—almost invariably the same thing happens. The tears suddenly break through, and the person will say, "You are the first person to really notice." And within minutes, as we talk about the important things, the cycle is ended there.

THE SURPRISE OF LONELINESS

Loneliness is perhaps the most unusual emotion produced by your grief recovery process. Why? Because beyond its unhealthy cycle, which you must somehow break, it also offers some surprises that are life-changing if embraced.

PAUSE TO REFLECT

*　∞　*

• How have you coped with your loneliness so far?
Physically:

_____

_____

_____

Emotionally:

_____

_____

_____

Why?

_____

_____

_____

Loneliness can be good. Let me explain how, and in so doing, also offer you the secret to the rest of your journey, and perhaps the rest of your life. These are not easy answers to your loneliness, but they are more than true—they can set you free.

Grasp these, however slowly, however much you can. If they seem too hard right now, reread them each time you pick up your workbook. Think about them one at a time, whenever you have a moment. But take a few steps now through this little area of your recovery road. You may find it's the way home.

Loneliness is the testing ground for our faith.

No one likes to be tested. Remember when your schoolteachers would spring a pop quiz on you? Do you recall ever being thankful for the test—especially when you didn't know it was coming? Did you even once say, "Oh thank you, gracious teacher, for the pop quiz today"? I rather doubt it.

Earlier, we explored the wise words Paul wrote to the Roman Christians: that endurance produces character, and character produces hope. In other words, a faith put to the test is a stronger, better faith. Yet we don't want our faith to be tested. We like it just the way it is. One of the sovereign ways that God chooses to build our faith, and ultimately, our character, is through the pathway of loneliness.

The concept with which we began this workbook—the image of your grief recovery process placing you in the middle of a "wilderness" from which you have to discover your recovery road—is a perfect image for this grief by-product. Wildernesses, by definition, are places of loneliness. But wildernesses, in life and in faith, are often places where our education deepens, our discovery expands, our knowledge grows.

The account of Christ's experience in the wilderness was preserved for us in the Bible. How did he deal with forty days and nights of utter loneliness? What was it like for Jesus to be lonely?

Christ suffered everything we suffer, the book of Hebrews tells us. Review Matthew's account of Jesus' temptation in the wilderness. Do you remember when his testing came? Jesus was at his weakest, physically and mentally. There must be a reason that tests come when we are at a low point.

That is exactly what happens to us during the grieving process. Loneliness comes when we are tested. And when we are tested, we have the chance to grow. To see it this way is to help understand your loneliness, even embrace it. I don't want to limit God, so I've learned how to accept the pathway or the wilderness experiences of loneliness.

And that's why the lonely part of the grieving process can be so critical. Sometimes God does not "fix" our grieving because he loves us. That's a hard pill to swallow sometimes, but if we never experience loneliness, we might never experience how God can fill us in a way nobody else can. If we never encounter pain, we will never experience or realize the awe of God, how he can come into a terrible, painful situation and meet our needs. If we never have fear in our lives, we will never be drawn into a place to rely upon God above all.

You see, I'm one of those crazy people who believes God is speaking all the time; we're just not dialed in. I'm like a radio, and sometimes I get off the station just a little. I believe

PAUSE TO REFLECT

- How can you see your loneliness as a faith-building test?

  _____

  _____

  _____

- What if your loneliness is a signal trying to get through? What could that message be?

  _____

  _____

  _____

- How can you tune in during your time of loneliness to what God might be saying through your grief?

  _____

  _____

  _____

we let the "white noise" created by everyday living block out God's still, small voice, which is always quietly transmitting. If you can believe that, then loneliness will almost become a joy, a time of dedicated—even hopeful—listening.

Loneliness is the place of true happiness.

Isn't that a hard one to swallow? Loneliness is…happiness?

I generally think of happiness as a party at which I have everything I want. But the Bible tells us that happiness is being content with what God has already provided for me.

Even my loneliness? Yes, even my loneliness, because in my loneliness God can teach me things that he can't teach me at any other time. And in my loneliness I may come to know God in a way that is unexplainable and yet exhilarating. A way that changes my perspective of my reason for living, that allows me to see my life in a God's-eye view—that changes even my definition of happiness.

> "I have learned the secret of being content in any and every situation….I can do everything through him who gives me strength."
>
> *Philippians 4:12-13*

Happiness isn't having everything I want. Happiness is wanting what I have right now. Happiness isn't a party as much as it is peace and joy. Would you agree? Happiness may be the moments of loneliness in which you learn something brand new about God's presence. As King David said, it may be a "seeking of God's face." It's possible. And so is your happiness.

SELF-CHECK

- Does God really want you to be happy? How do you know?

_____

Loneliness is a kind of dying we will all experience.

You can't get away from it. It's inescapable: You will feel lonely. Consider Jesus' experience. Christ was not exempt from loneliness, and neither are we. You could go everywhere Christ went. You could go to the wilderness, you could go to the Garden of Gethsemane, you could go to the cross—and you would find Jesus alone. He was the Son of God, yet he suffered. And so do we.

Do you know how gold ore becomes gold—the most precious of all earthly commodities? It's purified—plunged into fire to burn away all the things that keep it from being valuable. Like gold, we need to be refined by fire as well. The purifying is a kind of dying. And that sort of dying to our old selves comes, paradoxically, when we are all by ourselves.

This kind of dying must occur in our lives. If you consider your entire life so far, you will probably notice transitions. You are no longer the person that you were. The same is true in grief as it is in your walk of faith. Loneliness that comes from loss can be a time when we lose our own lives in a spiritual way. It gives us the time to leave the "ore" parts of our lives behind. Any kind of grief can have this effect. We come through it transformed, be it for good or for bad. Loneliness, the kind that draws us to God, can offer the kind of dying-to-self experience that creates a purer, more golden new you.

Loneliness is filled with choices.

The older I get, the less I want choices. I've had enough of them. I was in a restaurant the other day with a friend, and I literally told the waitress to order for me. Because I had so many choices in my life at that time, to even make a simple choice about lunch was too much for me.

When my wife and I go to a restaurant, I'll invariably ask her, "What are you going to have?" I'm not asking because I'm polite. I really want to know so I won't have to make the choice myself.

Loneliness also forces us to choose. We can choose the resentment, or we can choose God's way of endurance. When we are dealing with loss, the last thing we want is to be made to choose anything, much less something that affects us so deeply. The problem is, of course, that we don't consciously choose, usually. We unconsciously choose—we let it happen.

God gave you a free will. He's not going to force you to go on the path that he has provided for you. He's not going to make you agree with him that his way is a better way, and that the pain of your grief and loneliness can ultimately produce something better in your life. You can't hear him anyway. The pain is too loud.

But you do hit that crossroad. And now that you know it is there, you can consciously make the choice. Am I going to resist my loneliness and keep finding busy ways to fill this void in

> "Be faithful, even to the point of death, and I will give you the crown of life."
>
> *Revelation 2:10*

my life, or am I going to take the pathway of endurance? Do I choose resentment and bitterness, or the possibilities that time alone might mean for me spiritually?

When I walk in the forest I am faced with the choice of paths. One will quickly take me back to my home and to people. The other will take me farther into the woods, into a place of sanctuary with God—a place where you and I are never alone.

Choose endurance and watch the good that can come from it. Let your loneliness take you deeper into your spiritual walk. As you are alone and in pain right now, your heart probably feels like it is going to explode. I've had times in my life when I have been in large settings and felt that my heart was going to explode, with palpitations and profuse sweating. Clinically, we call it an anxiety attack. But knowing its name didn't stop it. You may know that feeling as well. You may have experienced it during your grief process. But even though you heart may pound, hold on.

You may say, "There's no hope. I just want to give up."

You can endure. You aren't alone. And you don't want to miss that crown of life.

STRATEGIES FOR LONELINESS

What can I do? you may be thinking. I want to give you five strategies for those moments when you feel all alone, your heart about to burst with the ache of it all.

Surrender the Loneliness

What does *surrender* mean? It doesn't mean giving up in the context of prayer. It means "giving over." If you surrender something in your possession, you are giving it to someone

SELF-CHECK

• Do you feel aimless in your loneliness? How might you change that feeling?

_____

_____

else. That's what you can do with your loneliness. Give it over in prayer to the One who will never leave you nor forsake you.

Prayer does not cost you a dime. The chat rooms and the 1-900 phone calls have nothing on prayer. Surrender your loneliness in an ongoing chat with God, and things will change. We can bring our loneliness to God. We can stop looking for all the other refuge points. Turn the phone off, turn the TV off, turn the radio off, and get alone with God. In that place, alone, is where we surrender. It's an act at the heart of the grief experience.

> None of us lives to himself alone and none of us dies to himself alone. If we live, we live to the Lord; and if we die, we die to the Lord. So, whether we live or die, we belong to the Lord.
>
> *Romans 14:7–8*

"Stop the world and let me off!" As I stood by a riverbank in Sacramento, banging my fist on the ground, that's what I once yelled at the top of my lungs. "This life is too hard right now. It's too much of a struggle. I just want to get off!" That used to be my prayer before I was a Christian. Now it's a whole new prayer: "Lord, this is your life in me. So I surrender my fears to you. I surrender my pain to you, and I even surrender my loneliness to you. You promised never to leave me nor forsake me. So, Lord, I belong to you. I'm here and I'm holding on."

Seek God

God is seeking you, so your next strategy when you are lonely is to seek God. It's what he wants. He wants you to shut off the rest of the world so he can be alone with you. Being alone is almost a misnomer, though, because you are never really alone. God is always with you. Tears are not forever. Your loneliness is not forever. God will bring you back to a place of comfort and joy.

God makes a place, a home, for the lonely, says Psalm 68:6. I love that word *home.* Notice the scripture doesn't say God is making a house. *House* has a cold feeling. *Home,* though, connotes love and warmth, a place of safety and refuge. It's a place with a warm fire and a nice comforter on the bed. It's a place that's been made a home by God.

> "I have been crucified with Christ and I no longer live, but Christ lives in me. The life I live in the body, I live by faith in the Son of God."
>
> *Galatians 2:20*

This verse alone is proof of the power of using your resource of resources—God's Word. If we search God's Word, we'll find comfort. How can God understand your loneliness? Hebrews tells us. It states that we have a God who is able to sympathize with our weaknesses, who puts nothing in our way, allowing us to accomplish the journey.

Submit to the Journey

The third thing that we can do with our loneliness is to submit to it and appreciate the journey. You are along for the ride of your life, but you have to make the choice to lean

> We do not have a high priest who is unable to sympathize with our weaknesses, but we have one who has been tempted in every way, just as we are—yet was without sin. Let us then approach the throne of grace with confidence, so that we may receive mercy and find grace to help us in our time of need.
>
> *Hebrews 4:15-16*

back into it, to stop fighting. There is no hope or peace until you come to that place of recognizing your helplessness. If you admit you cannot "fix" your loneliness yourself, then you position yourself to receive the fullness of God's grace and mercy. You may find that you come to the place where your loneliness becomes a gift, a treasured quiet time with God.

> God makes a home for
> the lonely.
>
> *Psalm 68:6 (NASB)*

God wastes nothing. Look at nature. What does a seed do? The seed dies and falls to the ground before anything new can happen. Only then does the cycle of life begin. Then the shoot grows up, becomes a stalk, then bears a flower. The flower has to die to bear the fruit, and then the fruit has to die to become a seed. The seed falls to start the cycle over again. Submit to the cycle of life and faith happening right now in you, and you will never be the same again. You will choose to be part of the process that God has so lovingly instilled in his natural world.

By the way, submission isn't a passive resignation. You can be along for the most natural ride of your life, but you still have steering—and growing—powers. Submission is really proactive. It's a time of testing and knowing God, of asking as you go, "How can God meet the need of this feeling of aloneness?

It's not saying: "I give up. That's just the way life is. I'm alone, and I'm going to be depressed about it." Rather, it's saying: "God I'm alone right now, and it hurts. But I'm open to whatever it is you want to do with this feeling. I'm here, and I know you're here with me."

SELF-CHECK

- Do you really trust that God will meet you in the middle of your loneliness, that he will bring about a change of feelings in your life?

_____

It is choosing to stay on the path when you could run for the barn.

Sometimes as I walk I come to a bench or a rock along the path that becomes a listening place for me and God. It took me a while to get used to sitting without a chair or blanket, risking dirtying my journey clothes or being close enough to the insects that could climb on me. But as I have sat there, I have come to the place of enjoying the loneliness. It is there that I have found God to be my Friend.

> Commit your way to the LORD;...he will make your righteousness shine like the dawn, the justice of your cause like the noonday sun. Be still before the LORD and wait patiently for him.
>
> *Psalm 37:5-7*

That's how it's possible to endure without bitterness. That's how to overcome your loneliness and even be surprised where it takes you down your grief recovery road.

Stick with It

The next strategy is a must: You have to stick with it. You must endure. The easiest way to be a victim of your loneliness is just to give up. If this is a problem for you, as it is for most people in grief recovery, remember that your urge to give up is probably not about your level of faith or your strength, but about your lack of energy due to the stress of your crisis. You are going through so much right now. Lapses will be common. Energy will dip. The best way to stick with it is found in one little word: *Wait.*

What do I mean? Waiting is trusting; it's dwelling, delighting, committing, It's turning from frustration and pity. And it's resting in the quiet of your solitude that can come only in your loneliness.

A key term in your wait is "commit," as you can see in Psalm 37:5-7. A commitment to waiting for the surprises found in your loneliness—in waiting on God there—can be pivotal in conquering the pain of your grief's loneliness. It's not searching out how many groups you can join or finding busywork to fill your day, but committing to dwell and delight in his ways, to spend time with God and let him minister to you, and to commit to whatever time it takes.

That's the God that we're waiting upon. That's the God that changes your loneliness into "aloneness" with him. It is amazing how much more I see when I wait: The squirrels play tag in the trees; the doe and the fawns eat fresh blackberries; and the buck scrapes the fuzz off of his antlers.

Serve Others Who Grieve

The last strategy to conquer loneliness is to serve. I can hear you now: "Serve who? I'm lonely here. In fact, I've isolated myself, which has made me even more alone. So how will I serve anyone else? There's nobody around."

If you are feeling like that, you won't be able to serve anyone else, nor will you have any desire to. First, you will have to discover the surprising, good side of loneliness that nurtures you instead of isolates you.

> "Since ancient times no one has heard, no ear has perceived, no eye has seen any God besides you, who acts on behalf of those who wait for him. You come to the help of those who gladly do right, who remember your ways."
>
> *Isaiah 64:4-5*

When you begin to experience that surprise, then, instead of being worried about the negative effects of lingering loneliness, listen closely. God may be saying, "Get out of yourself. Serve others around you."

"But I can't, I can't," you may say. And you'd be right. But God in his mercy, love, and grace has given you the same opportunity to turn your pain into something wonderful as he gave missionary Elisabeth Elliot.

Elliot has written more than twenty books. I can only imagine the millions of people around the world who have been inspired from what has been produced through her pain. Suppose she had decided to become bitter and isolated, never discovering the surprising joy of loneliness. Suppose she had decided not to endure. The gift that God had for us through her life would never have been shared. In her endurance, she has given. In her endurance, we have all received. In *The Path of Loneliness* she wrote, "I actually believed that widowhood was a gift from God, and I was able to offer it back to God as an act of worship. I was able to thank God, knowing that Jim was with the Lord."

Praise be to the God and Father of our Lord Jesus Christ, the Father of compassion and the God of all comfort, who comforts us in all our troubles, so that we can comfort those in any trouble with the comfort we ourselves have received from God. For just as the sufferings of Christ flow over into our lives, so also through Christ our comfort overflows.

2 Corinthians 1:3–5

SELF-CHECK

- What have you learned so far in your grief recovery that you might want to share with someone else going through loss?

_____

_____

_____

Recently, I talked to a man who has come through his painful grief journey in a wonderful way. I said to him, "You're very healthy. You are saying all the right things, you look good, and you seem to have made your way through recovery and healing."

"You're right," he smiled, and then added, "now I'm ready to start serving." He had captured one of the major healthy grief recovery results. Ultimately, we come to the place where we realize through the pain of these emotions—through journeying through loneliness, through learning about anger, through acknowledging our guilt, through experiencing the processes of grief—that we have learned something valuable. Now we can lead others to the trailhead, encouraging them on their journey.

Work It Out

1. Have you surrendered your loss to God? If not, how might you do so now?

_____

_____

_____

2. How have you handled your loneliness so far?

_____

_____

_____

3. Has there been a moment in your loneliness that you felt more "alone" than "lonely"? What does that mean to you?

_____

_____

_____

4. How might you practice experiencing the presence of God in your loneliness?

_____

_____

5. How can you endure without bitterness? What have you found helpful from this chapter?

_____

_____

_____

Grief Recovery Journal

Date _____

Dear _____ :

This is how I feel right now:

_____

_____

_____

_____

_____

_____

_____

_____

_____

_____

_____

This is what I've discovered today:

_____

_____

_____

_____

_____

_____

_____

_____

_____

_____

_____

This is what I still question today:

_____

_____

_____

_____

_____

_____

_____

_____

_____

Extra space to finish your thoughts, if needed:

_____

_____

_____

_____

_____

_____

_____

_____

_____

_____

For additional encouragement, listen to
Number 8 on the *Grief Recovery Workbook CD*

Chapter 8

Guilt: *"If Only..."*

Charles was a strong Christian businessman. He was a man's man. He was tall, handsome, drove an expensive car, owned a nice house, owned his own business, and was an avid sportsman. If you were struggling, Charles was the man to go see. He would give you the shirt off his back. Literally. He was well known for his generosity and for giving back to the community. He was a board member of a large Christian church in the community and provided scholarships for children to its Christian school. But Charles found himself in some financial trouble in his business, and, for whatever reason, he could not cope with it. He drove to Yosemite National Park and took his own life, leaving a wife, three children, and many shocked friends behind. I was called in to help his loved ones deal with what he did and with suicide's unique grief recovery issues.

With a suicide, guilt rules the day. Everyone blames themselves. No one is really responsible except the person who took his own life, but all his loved ones will, without fail, blame themselves. Why they do so is interesting. Every suicidal case I've worked, this has happened. When all those who loved the suicide victim are sitting in a room together, grieving, comparing notes, they can see clearly that the person gave clear signs of being suicidal. But suicide victims don't bring all the people they know together in one room and say, "I'm suicidal." They gave Mom the *S*; they gave Dad the *U*. They gave Sister the *I*, the best friend the *C*, and the co-worker got the *I*. They gave the bill collector the *D*

and their doctor the *E*. But when it's too late, the loved ones realize that the actions altogether spell suicide. And that's when everyone guiltily thinks, *Why didn't we see it?* For
Charles' family and friends this was no different, and yet through the lessons that follow,
they were able to process their guilt on their unique journey of grief.

Guilt is not reserved for the fallout after suicides. Any loss's grief recovery process will
have its share of guilt. I have seen it pop up in every situation imaginable. Guilt trips seem
to take us everywhere.

Like most of the other major emotions we've explored, guilt also exists for a good
and healthy purpose. It's an emotion that God gave us to keep us thinking about our
behavior. It serves as a day-to-day moral compass. Guilt is that emotion that reminds us
to stop doing potentially harmful activities. It helps keep our freedom—our free will—
in check so that we resist potentially harmful situations. It can keep us from making bad
decisions.

But that's not the type of guilt you experience in your loss. Yours is the kind that
makes you feel as if you could have prevented a suicide, or could have helped a terminally
ill person some better way, or could have even saved a child from an accident. It's the kind
that makes you feel as if you caused a divorce. The kind that comes from believing someone's accusations of your part in a tragedy. The kind of guilt that creeps in during the
grieving process and says, "What if…" or "If only…" It's the kind that is hard to deal with,
since capturing its exact nature is difficult.

Guilt can be a debilitating emotion. It's a tiny, gnawing voice in your ear, accusing
you deservedly or not. To overcome your feelings of guilt, you'll first have to understand
them and determine why you are so susceptible to them. Let's look at where guilt origi-
nates in your life and why.

THE SOURCES OF GUILT

Actual Wrongs

Guilt can come from actual wrongdoing. Anyone can make a mistake. Everyone can
make bad choices. What we do affects not only ourselves, but others, no matter what happens. In other words, sometimes people *are* guilty. Good people *can* do harmful things.

Drunk drivers kill innocent people. A husband can be unfaithful to his wife. A man can make wrong choices in his business and feel so guilty that suicide seems the only option. Guilt itself can be a killer. And at the very least, if left untended, it can cripple a good person for life.

Years ago, I was called to help a grieving mother whose baby had died at daycare. The daycare operator was charged with the child's murder. My wife, Cathy, was talking to the mother one day, and a whole other story unfolded. The mother began telling a story she never told the police. The mother had had time to think, to find her moral compass. She had been late for work that day, giving the baby a bath in the sink. She became frustrated, pushed the baby, and accidentally made him hit his head on the sink. She took her son on to the daycare operator, dropped him off, and thirty minutes later he was dead. The daycare operator was on trial for her life, and yet it was the mother who actually was guilty of the injuries. Cathy convinced her that she had to tell the district attorney the truth. Ultimately, the daycare operator was freed and the mother was never charged.

So, sometimes, our guilt is valid, and we have to find ways of coping with the reality of it. Other times, it is a hangover emotion—a trip that we send ourselves on, or a trip that others send us on.

Guilt Trips

Often, we aren't really guilty of anything, but we regret not having done something. It is the guilt of things I should have said; the things I wish I'd done.

What if...

If only...

What I could have done...

What I should have done...

Hindsight is 20/20. It is the guilt created by unrealistic expectations. Maybe you felt more relief than grief at your loved one's funeral. Maybe the loved one died of a long illness or a protracted aging process, and maybe you are glad the suffering is over. While everyone else is crying around you, you are dry-eyed. And that feeling confuses you; it seems wrong, and you feel guilty. That is only one kind of guilt trip possible in your life right now because of your loss.

You have no reason to feel guilty, yet guilt is screaming accusations in your ear. A common mental "loop" in a tragedy is the one many workers at the World Trade Center disaster dealt with—a rescuer-savior complex in which they believe they could have and should have done more: "If we did our jobs, why were so many unaccounted for? Why couldn't we recover all of them?" Many firefighters who were at the World Trade Center on 9/11 and beyond experienced the same guilt. Even me. Yet in reality we did all we could. There is no more unjustified guilt trip than this. And yet we have all experienced this false sense of guilt.

Are you starting to see the picture? Let's look at another.

Is this you? *I did everything I could; I was at her bedside through all kinds of treatment. I fed her, I bathed her, I stayed up all hours; I read the Scriptures; I prayed with her. Why do I feel like I should have done more?*

As I mentioned earlier, people who are dealing with a loved one's terminal illness, such as AIDS or cancer, should keep a diary or journal about what they are doing to alleviate the guilt that will invariably come later. The Actions Timeline tool in chapter 3 is meant to help remind a person who did not keep such a journal of the truth.

Then, there are guilt trips that society gives us—those that make unrealistic demands on us. Socially we are bombarded with feelings of small daily guilt trips. How can we not feel guilty? We are made to feel guilty over such things as whether we should eat that candy bar or whether we should give money to a charity that has employed a telemarketer to "reach out and touch" us. You could be having a great day, until somebody says, "Oh, you really should have done this a little better," or "If only you had done that, everything would have worked." Or the worst: "I told you so." The message you really hear is: *I don't measure up.*

I can hear you now: "But you don't know me. You don't know what I've done. I should have known better. I'm not what God wants me to be." Are you so sure that these aren't false expectations? Daily, we are bombarded socially by feelings of guilt. How can we not feel guilty?

Moral Compass

A moral compass—the side of guilt that prevents bad decisions—reminds us of boundaries and keeps us from abusing our freedoms, which will prevent us from inflicting pain on ourselves and others. "I'll feel guilty if I have that affair." "I'll feel guilty if I steal." "I'll feel guilty if I don't treat my neighbors as myself." So to avoid having that lousy feeling about ourselves, we make the moral decision.

So, like all of our other emotions—even pain— guilt has spiritual potential. A godly guilt—our moral compass—guides us through life and points us back in the right direction when we fail. That's when the truth of God's thumbprint on us, our conscience, draws us back to a relationship with God.

> You, dear children,
> are from God and
> have overcome them,
> because the one
> who is in you is
> greater than the one
> who is in the world.
>
> *1 John 4:4*

Guilt of any kind indicates the need for a recalibration of our lives. This is one of those emotions that can be a dashboard warning light. We need to ask ourselves when we feel guilty, "Is this good guilt? Is it positive guilt that can help me reconsider my actions, or is it negative guilt that will do nothing but tear me down?"

THE WRONG WAYS WE DEAL WITH GUILT

Running

The first reaction to that guilt feeling is to run from it. It's a time-honored, though futile, coping mechanism. The book of Genesis records the first such reaction to guilt feelings (Genesis 3:6-13). Adam and Eve showed us a classic illustration of how humans have always dealt with guilt. If you'll recall, after realizing they had disobeyed God, they ran away. Their thinking must have been just like ours: *If I can't be found, then maybe this guilt feeling will go away and I won't have to face it.*

How do we run away? We isolate ourselves—sometimes to the point of being rude to anyone who attempts to help us—because it's too painful to face that feeling of guilt.

I've often seen this dynamic be the true reason that marriages collapse. Neither spouse

PAUSE TO REFLECT

CREATE A TIMELINE

As mentioned in chapter 3, during a long illness or hospitalization I often encourage loved ones to keep a journal of the process—to recall all the trips to the doctor, all the changing of bed linens, all the medication-giving, all the long nights, all the services rendered to the loved one and the things endured—to help with the guilt that will inevitably follow.

But during grief recovery, you have the exercise as one of your recovery tools. Why not use it now? A timeline can be almost as helpful in bringing the experience and your participation in it back into proper perspective: your efforts to fight the disease with your mate; the steps you took to keep the relationship together; and exercise and diet regimens you kept to in order to stay healthy.

Below, create a timeline of your loss. On the horizontal line, put the months or weeks that passed. Then, on the vertical lines along the chart, jot down the things you did for the loved one along the way. Use the small one in the space below or the larger one in chapter 3.

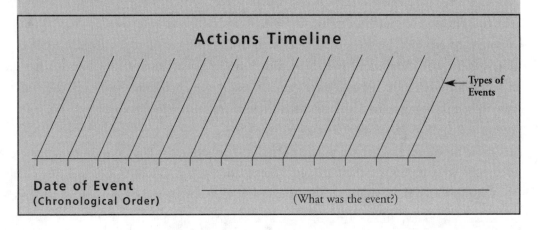

Actions Timeline

Types of Events

Date of Event
(Chronological Order)

(What was the event?)

wants a divorce, but sometimes the tremendous guilt from the unfaithful partner is so great that he or she will run for relief from his or her own feelings of guilt. In my experience, I've found that if I can help the unfaithful spouse cope with the guilt and the pressure that was brought into the relationship, the marriage has a chance.

Hiding

The second reaction is hiding, just as Adam and Eve also did. Our ways of hiding, though, are much more sophisticated. We will hide behind substance abuse, medicating ourselves with prescription drugs, street drugs, alcohol, food—whatever we can find. We'll numb ourselves to a point where we can't feel the emotion anymore. Sometimes, the hiding becomes a form of self-destruction or self-punishment. We may feel like we deserve to die, and this sort of substance abuse is a slow form of suicide.

But believe this: You may have faced a tragic event, and maybe something disastrous happened, but God doesn't want you to die. And he doesn't want you to run away from the feelings of guilt.

Adam and Eve not only hid, they were hiding from God. Sometimes that's the kind of hiding we also do: "God surely won't approve of what I did, so I'll ignore him, hoping he'll ignore me." Why do we do this? I think it's because we really don't have a proper perspective of who God is and how much he loves us. But if our view of God sees him as all wrath and judgment and no love, all lightning bolts and no compassion, we're missing out on so much.

Blaming

The third reaction to feelings of guilt is to blame others. Adam and Eve also dealt with their guilt in this unhealthy way. They blamed everyone but themselves. Even when it is all our own fault, we will almost always look for someone else to blame. Adam blamed Eve. Eve blamed the serpent. No one took personal responsibility. Rationalization seems to soften the sharp edges of our guilt. We think: *If they hadn't done this, I wouldn't have done that, so it's really not all my fault.*

Children are naturals at this way of dealing with guilt, aren't they? We've all heard the following:

"I wouldn't have punched her in the eye if she hadn't called me a name!"

"Well, I wouldn't have called him a name if he hadn't teased me!"

We parents are constantly challenged with forcing our children to take personal responsibility for their actions and stop the blame game. And yet we find it easy to take some comfort in the tried-and-true blame method ourselves when faced with our own guilt.

Since Adam and Eve, nothing has changed. We still run and hide, and we still blame. But all these ways of coping with our guilt deny us the education and the experiences that God has for us. We need not handle it the way Adam and Eve did. There's another, better way of overcoming guilt and staying on your road to grief recovery.

THE ANTIDOTE FOR GUILT

Reassess

There are really only two kinds of guilt: justified and unjustified. We need to keep reminding ourselves that guilt can come from small things as well as big, from things not done as well as things done, from real situations and imagined ones. That's why it is such a slippery emotion to deal with. It can also come riding piggyback with someone else's wrong choices. One example I've seen far too often happens in marriages. The husband has a failure of his inner moral compass and has an affair with another woman. His guilt is justified. But then, his wife begins to feel guilty herself. Surely her husband wouldn't have had that affair if she had been more attractive or less judgmental. Or she could name a thousand other reasons his moral failure was her fault. What kind of guilt is that? Unjustified guilt.

How do you recognize whether a guilt feeling is justified or unjustified? Is that feeling positive guilt, meant to help guide you in a straight path through life, or is it negative guilt feeling which does nothing but tear you down? I have found a way to help distinguish the two kinds of guilt.

Unjustified guilt is what I call "condemnation." Condemnation is a broken record, a punishing replaying of the consequences of a bad choice.

Justified guilt is what I call "conviction." Conviction leads to repentance of a bad choice or a sin, and it invites a brand-new start with God. Repentance means to turn away from the wrong and head in another direction. That is always God's plan for con-viction—repentance, reconciliation, and restoration.

So, which voice am I hearing? That's the question to ask. Try this test to apply to your guilt, be it imagined or real:

Ask yourself, *Does this feeling of guilt draw me into a closer relationship with God? Does this allow me to move past my circumstance, past my trial, past my failure, past my error?*

If the answer is no, then your guilt is unjustified guilt. If the answer is yes, then it's justifiable guilt. You are only an acknowledgment away from being back in a healthy rela-tionship with God, and in a position to begin to rebound.

Justified guilt keeps pointing you toward forgiveness. If you don't take this step, you'll find yourself talking to God about whatever you may or may not have done wrong—over and over. Three weeks later, a month later, even years later, you're still deal-ing with your guilt, asking God for forgiveness for something that's already been for-given long ago.

Unjustified guilt will always lead you to your supposed failures and keeps you focused on them. It never allows you a breath of fresh air. It never allows you to get up and start walking again. The source can be society. It can be other people, who keep heaping guilt on you even after you've said you're sorry. Or you could be doing this to your-self. If you can't ever feel the guilt lift, even after you've taken it to God, then you are laboring under unjustified guilt. And it's time to let it go.

> Joshua was dressed in filthy clothes as he stood before the angel. The angel said to those who were standing before him, "Take off his filthy clothes." Then he said to Joshua, "See, I have taken away your sin, and I will put rich garments on you."
>
> *Zechariah 3:3-4*

Guilt can make us feel filthy like Joshua did before the angel of God (Zechariah 3:3-4). We feel like we are dressed in filthy rags. But the moment we come to God, what does he say? As it was for Joshua, it is for us—the filthy rags vanish and all we find are "rich garments" instead. That's a great image about a great truth.

The longer those recordings play and the longer you hear that voice of accusation, the more it has a hold in your life. If you can catch it now, the first few times it plays, the easier it is to rid yourself of its incessant whisper.

One of the best ways to catch it is with God's Word. If you don't know what God's Word says, then you are not tapping into truth and healing words. There are over three hundred references to guilt in the Bible. Scripture does not take this subject lightly. Yet once we want to be free of it, we can be totally free of it, justified or unjustified. Read and then reread Romans 5:1-2, the passage that Paul wrote to the Roman Christians who were struggling with the same feelings you have. That's your ticket home from your guilt trip.

> Since we have been justified through faith, we have peace with God through our Lord Jesus Christ, through whom we have gained access by faith into this grace in which we now stand. And we rejoice in the hope of the glory of God.
>
> *Romans 5:1-2*

Acknowledge

Talk it out with a trusted friend. Often, a powerful antidote to guilt is talking about it with somebody who is close to you. Our perspective is so off-center after a crisis. Often when we feel guilty, we start redefining the event and our part in it. Our sense of reality escapes us. I think this is especially true when a loss has come after a loved one's long illness. The "if onlys" are almost irrepressible after terminal illnesses or avoidable accidents.

My wife felt it when her father died after going through months of chemotherapy. As she flew back and forth to be with him, sometimes that unjustified guilt would creep in. She could not get rid of thoughts such as: *If only I had taken him to another doctor.* Or, *Maybe I should have done something different. Maybe it would have been easier for him if only…*

When she finally admitted her feelings to me during that stressful time, I was surprised.

"Don't you remember how many times you went back?" I said to her. "Don't you remember that you stayed for weeks?" And then I listed all the things she had done to be faithful and helpful during the entire illness.

"That's right," she finally acknowledged, and all that unjustified guilt faded away. So, talking with someone can help you get the proper perspective.

Often you can feel guilt because you don't believe you are grieving "properly" or appear "socially acceptable" after such an experience, as mentioned at the beginning of this chapter. After a terminal illness ends in death for someone you love, you may feel a tremendous relief. Everyone else is crying and weeping at the funeral while you may be glad that your loved one isn't suffering anymore. This is a normal response, largely because you have been journeying the grief pathway throughout the event. At the moment of diagnosis you entered the forest, and now at your loved one's "graduation," you are well down the road while others are just starting to walk it.

Claim God's Promises

Claiming Scripture promises is a sure-fire antidote for guilt. Complete the Pause to Reflect activity below, reading the verses, then summarizing them in the lines that follow or in your journal pages at the end of this chapter.

PAUSE TO REFLECT

Read the following passages aloud and briefly record what you learn from them:

1 John 3:20 _____

1 John 2:1 _____

Romans 8:1 _____

Psalm 32:3-5 _____

1 John 1:9 _____

Move On

What if you really did do something you feel is justifiably wrong? God already knows the truth. He isn't waiting for your confession before he flips the lightning bolt switch. If he wanted to hit you with those lightning bolts, he could have done it a long time ago. Then my question is, Why run?

Confession is when we agree with God about the wrongness of what we did, then we move on, being open, allowing for the character-building that is always another step down the recovery road.

God stays with us during our failures, wanting to use our shortcomings and failures as well as our talents and virtues. And then God wants us to know that we can start again.

David, whose guilt was often justified, knew something you need to know right now. When he wrote, "When I kept silence, my bones wasted away," he didn't say his bones will waste away or his bones could waste away. He said his bones did waste away. But the promise was still there. Even if you feel you have been hiding something for years, there is still the joy that will come from getting it out and acknowledging it, so you can move on.

When I think of this promise of God, I always think about the children of Israel. Despite their rebellion and their failures, the Lord delivered them from the Red Sea, provided manna and quail, and yet they rebelled against him, whining and making idols. And in all of that, God still called them his chosen, beloved people. If I were God, those lightning bolts would have been constantly flying. Yet Israel's cycle of failure, rebellion, discipline, and reunion kept going 'round and 'round in the Bible, waiting to be read by us.

> "When I kept silent, my bones wasted away."
>
> *Psalm 32:3*

And that is probably why we have these stories—to show us this very pattern so we understand. Through all our failures, there can always be renewal and hope. God didn't forsake the Hebrews, and he hasn't left us. He uses our mistakes to educate us, to teach us godly principles, to build godly character, to refine and draw us closer into a more intimate relationship with him. Whatever the source of your guilt, the solution is found in him. Leave your guilt here, and move on down your road to grief recovery. And remember, if you acknowledge your guilt to God, he is faithful to forgive you of the sin and cleanse you of all the unrighteousness associated with the behavior.

Work It Out

Catch your guilt now—analyze it, label it, and overcome it.

Use this exercise to think about your feelings of guilt—justified or unjustified. Consider each point and how it impacts how you are feeling and whether or not you are continuing your recovery.

1. What do you feel guilty about?

_____

_____

_____

2. What kind of guilt is this: justified or unjustified? Circle the statements below that apply to this feeling you're having.

Unjustified Guilt

- Comes from condemnation, not conviction
- Remains long after you've acknowledged it
- Focuses on your failures
- Leads away from recovery and a spiritual walk

Justified Guilt

- Comes from conviction, not condemnation
- Is identified by your moral compass
- Points you back to repentance, reconciliation, and restoration with God

Think hard. Then write what you have learned about the guilt you are feeling here and in your journal pages that follow.

_____

_____

Grief Recovery Journal

Date _____

Dear _____ :

This is how I feel right now:

_____

_____

_____

_____

_____

_____

_____

_____

_____

This is what I've discovered today:

_____

_____

_____

_____

_____

_____

_____

_____

_____

This is what I still question today:

_____

_____

_____

_____

_____

_____

_____

_____

_____

_____

_____

Extra space to finish your thoughts, if needed:

_____

_____

_____

_____

_____

_____

_____

_____

_____

_____

For additional encouragement, listen to Number 9 on the *Grief Recovery Workbook CD*

Chapter 9

Pain: Thorns and Blessings

A friend who recently died of breast cancer after a nine-year battle was one of the most courageous women I've ever known. She had been diagnosed at thirty-four years of age. She gave herself a goal: She wanted to see her four-year-old daughter graduate from high school. That was her only request. Throughout the nine years, even though she attempted every answer modern medicine offered, she was in constant pain. She was in emotional pain, realizing that each second was one less moment she would have with her family. She was in spiritual pain, attempting to understand how God could be in a situation which would leave her child motherless just when she needed her most. She was in physical

> "Hear, O LORD, and be merciful to me;
> O LORD, be my help."
>
> *Psalm 30:10*

pain, causing her even more distress because she knew it was taking away the quality of those remaining seconds to be her daughter's mother.

And yet, through all that anguish, she never gave in to the pain. She arrived at the school every day to volunteer. She was the mother who was on every field trip. She was sewing and knitting until all hours of the night to make costumes for school productions. She led a church choir. And then when her daughter was in the sixth grade, she began losing her battle with cancer. Even her courage and defiance of her pain couldn't stop the spread of the disease.

The daughter grew up watching her mother's struggle with the grief process, thrust upon her by the loss of her health. After her mother died, how did the daughter handle her death? This is what she said to me: "I'm going to be okay. Mom's not suffering anymore. And I wouldn't want her to suffer another day just so she could see me graduate." The child's loss process had been going on as long as her mother's. And now, although it sounded strange, she was well along her recovery road.

Grief is universal. It is not reserved for any particular group of people. Pain knows no boundaries, be it age or geography or culture. It affects each of us who are part of the human race.

On an October day, I arrived at the home of Lisa. Her husband, Richard, had chased his dreams from Manchester, England, to Sacramento to marry her and fly helicopters. While training a man who had come from Japan to learn to fly, Richard's copter crashed in a field near Napa, California. Richard was killed instantly in the fire of the wreckage. His young bride was devastated by the loss of her Prince Charming. His family rushed from their home in England to be by her side.

The young Japanese man was burned over 70 percent of his body. He survived at a local intensive care unit at the medical center for months. His parents came from Japan, speaking little to no English. I and a chaplain named Martha would go every day to visit and share the love of God with the family, bowing and never looking them right in the eye. The man died when a breathing tube was removed that tore his artery.

After conducting a service for Richard, his father and uncle approached me with tears in their eyes, saying, "You must come. You must come." They were inviting me to return to England with them to perform the same service for hundreds of family members there. Cathy and I flew there and ministered to many people in Richard's homeland.

The family from Japan offered me the greatest honor a non-Shinto, non-Japanese person could be given: I was asked to handle the man's cremation. As I stood at the solemn ceremony with only mother and father and the hot embers of their son, I had no language to speak to them with, just understanding and sensitivity.

At the end of the ceremony, they turned to me, bowed a last time, put their hands together, and motioned to me that it was time for me to pray for them and their son. What a privilege! A final placement of the bones, a sealing of the urn, and then the final wrapping of the porcelain jar with a fine silk scarf that the mother had worn the entire time.

Watching families work through their grief has taught me that after a loss, everything hurts. This pain is a normal part of the grief process. Pain can be both physical and emotional.

The pain you are living with daily must feel like thistles across your road to recovery. Sometimes when I walk I wander off the trail for some observation—perhaps to follow a flock of turkeys or get a closer look at a beautiful buck. But I always pay a price for this upclose-and-personal observation: I get burrs in my shoes. Typically returning to the trail to continue the journey, I must stop to deal with the pain.

You have started and made some wonderful observations. You may have wandered deep into the adventure and off the trail, exposing yourself to the pain. Now you have to deal with the burrs before moving on in the journey. We must choose to address the burrs in our shoes if we are to successfully navigate the road to recovery. Let's look at the purpose of pain to understand its importance in our grief process.

THE THORN'S ROLE

At our house we have some beautiful rosebushes. I always appreciate the smell of the roses, the beauty of the roses—the yellows, the platinums, the reds, and the purples. They're just so gorgeous. But what I don't appreciate about the roses are the thorns. Not long ago, as I was taking down our Christmas lights, I truly did not appreciate the thorns. Whenever you're around a rosebush, have you noticed that no matter how hard you try, those thorns just find you? They found me. My first thought after the pain was, *Why did God put thorns on roses? Why do the most beautiful flowers on the face of the earth have thorns?* I had never questioned why God made roses, but I definitely questioned why God made thorns.

The natural world teaches us so many life lessons. *The thorns must be there to protect the rose's beauty,* I realized. But my question really wasn't about roses or thorns. My question was about the very essence of crisis work—your pain. Why is there pain in our lives? Why do we suffer? How could thorns in our lives be for our good?

Pain Protects Us

Sooner or later, we're going to have some kind of joy happen in our lives. Sooner or later, we're going to have some kind of pain happen in our lives as well.

But just as thorns are on a rose to protect it, so is pain part of our lives to protect us in some way. Physical pain protects us by letting us know when something is wrong in our bodies. Studies have been done on people who don't feel pain due to various unusual reasons. The findings seem to indicate that they are much more susceptible to harm than the rest of us. If a person doesn't feel his hand burning, how will he know to move it away from the fire? His life may depend on that pain. Increasing pain from a wound may signal to us that it is getting infected, worsening, or endangering the health of the whole body.

I once read a book about a doctor who worked with leprosy patients. One of his comments has stayed with me: "They only wish that they could have pain." The disease can get so bad that sufferers don't feel anything—except for their mental anguish.

I appreciated pain when my wife was thrown from a horse. As I rushed to help her, I remember thinking, *Is she alive? Is she dead?* Then I heard her. She was in pain, lots of it. And at that second, I was very appreciative that she had pain. First, it told me that she was alive. Second, it told me that she was conscious and alert so we would be able to communicate. And third, it told me that she still had sensation. The more pain she felt in her legs and her feet, the less chance the fall had caused any paralysis. So while it may not be pleasant, as my wife can tell you, pain is meant to get our attention, to warn us, and even to keep us alive. Our bodies are built so pain is actually protection, a very loud early-warning signal.

Pain Builds Character

"No pain, no gain" is the old sports saying. It may sound awful and even cruel, but it's the same way in life. We may wish it weren't true, but growth often comes through crisis. Character is built through problems. Walking through the fire purifies. And as hard as it may sound right now, pain plays a large part in life's lessons. Our response to it can either make us or break us, and the good news is that God offers enough strength to make it through. In fact, that's been his plan all along.

As you move through your grief, you will want to do anything in your power to get rid of the pain, the heartache radiating unbearably throughout the rest of the body. Yet it's at that place, right there, that God wants to build godly character in your life. Through endurance he builds character, and then through character we gain hope, Scripture tells us. And *hope will not disappoint us* as we walk through this journey!

Pain is a tough benefit to our bodies. It focuses our attention; it offers warning signs. It reminds us of our vulnerability and shows our need for a God who wipes away all tears (Isaiah 25:8). If you let it, pain will produce a new you, full of deep character and new hope. "If I persevere, I'm going to be a person of deeper character," you can tell yourself with confidence. "And through my deeper character, I will be filled with a brand-new hope."

> "The Sovereign LORD
> will wipe away the tears
> from all faces."
>
> *Isaiah 25:8*

Attitude Affects the Level of Pain

I can hear you now: "Okay, I understand what pain is, and I am trying to be open to its role from God's point of view. But that doesn't help the physical pain I'm feeling right at this very minute. What can I do right now as I work through all this? Anything?"

Be it a death, a divorce, separation, abandonment, the loss of a limb, the loss of a job, the loss of a child, or the loss of trust, we may feel physical pain through the process, but it will be coming from emotional pain. But you can gain back a bit of control as you move toward recovery. How? Your attitude will affect the level of pain that you will experience.

Though it's hard to grasp when you're in the grip of pain, your attitude about it is incredibly important in its management. If you have the right attitude, you can tolerate it long enough to work through it and see the good that it may foster. And you'll notice that just as a muscle gets stronger the more often it's used, so will your attitude.

It's rather like getting a splinter in your finger. If you're like me, the first few times you had to deal with using something sharp to pull it out, you almost freaked out. That feeling quadrupled the first time I had to remove a splinter from my child's tiny finger. Suddenly that splinter was as big as a log. But my attitude changed once I'd done that a few times in my life. It was still painful, but I handled it better. Now, especially since my children are older and more active, I have had lots of practice at pulling out splinters. I just get the tweezers out and do what I have to do. I have a whole different attitude about the very same pain.

It's amazing how our attitude affects the level of pain that we experience. If we have a bad attitude about it, if we look at pain as being an enemy, any pain-producing situation will overwhelm, overtake, and consume us. Our pain is enhanced. Yet if we look at pain as part of a loss process—and more importantly, a part of the growing process with God—then we can see it as a learning journey. Any loss produces "thorns." They are deeply emotional. And the emotional response to your loss's thorns can intensify your fear, anger, guilt, and loneliness. But they can be handled. And our attitude toward them will affect the level of pain that we experience.

It's important that you understand this: Your grief's emotions can enhance your pain or pacify it. When you feel those strong emotions, the emotional pain enhances them, intensifies, makes them worse. If you deal with the pain, you are saying to yourself that you will be able to manage the fear. If you deal with the pain, you can manage the anger. If you deal with the pain, you can manage the guilt.

If you don't deal with your pain—if you don't stop and get the thistles out of your shoes—you not only can't continue to experience the journey, but these strong emotions remain in control. Then you can't manage your guilt, you can't manage your anger, you can't manage your fear, you can't manage your guilt or loneliness. Your emotions can become more significant in your life than the loss itself. The result is that your tragedy becomes not only an end to a relationship, but also an end to your future. If you are not careful to deal with what is creating the emotional pain, then all the other built-in indicators from God can get way out of sync, and you are stuck on that emotional roller coaster that never ends.

Attitude is about viewing your loss through new lenses, seeing it from a God's-eye view, as talked about throughout this workbook. If you don't form the right perspective of pain—why you experience it and how you can grow through it—then almost invariably you will develop bitterness toward God. And this will only make the pain worse. Your loss cannot change, but your attitude about its place in your life can.

So how do you develop this healthier attitude about your pain? There are two ways—our way and God's way. Let's explore both.

SELF-CHECK

- What thorn is bothering you right now?

_____

- What might you be doing to make your pain more intense?

_____

HOW TO HANDLE THE THORNS

There are two reactions you can have to the pain coming from your loss. There is the human way and God's way. First, let's look at our way—the human way.

• Our Way—Insulation and Isolation

One of our primary ways to deal with pain is to insulate—to pretend that the pain doesn't exist and that it doesn't hurt us. We pull on those insulated gloves, and we think those thorns can't touch us. _I'm not going to let pain touch my life. If I don't have to deal with it I'll be okay._ Just because we put the gloves on and can touch the rose, the thorns don't go away, do they? Instead, our attempts to insulate ourselves from the pain set in motion a series of destructive events.

We lie to ourselves. We fill the void and try to numb the pain with anything that works, and that almost always involves self-destructive behavior. Alcohol and drug abuse are the most common responses. But we can also pacify our pain with toxic relationships and actions. We may find ourselves doing things we thought we could never do. And then, because we don't want to face the pain of what we've done, we deceive ourselves: "I didn't do that. And even if I did, it's not that bad." Then we have to lie to others, so we set in process a series of events over which we have little control. We find ourselves in a cycle of temptation and accusation and deception. And the worst part is, the thistles are still there. Putting on two pairs of socks doesn't cause the pain to go away; it doesn't take the burrs out of your shoes. They are always there.

I find it interesting to work with people who have dealt with their pain in an insulating way. I can see layers of protective devices that they have built around their pain. And *those* layers are almost always protected with a veneer of anger and bitterness. And then it takes a long process to get down to the real problem. Many people even deny being angry, the insulation is so thick.

Some people are good at covering up pain with humor. Problems? Not me. Everything is a joke. These people can look wonderful, but when you take a close look into their lives, you find deep pain. But just like a splinter you ignore, the longer you don't deal with it, the more infected it can become. And the only way to fix it is to dig down and pull it out. Only later, it's going to hurt a lot more.

The second way that humans deal with pain is to isolate. If we don't have to deal with other people, surely the pain will go away. We make ourselves invisible. We withdraw emotional energy from those closest to us—spouse, friend, family member, a community in general. Men do this in their marriages much more than women. They withdraw from their wives when there's pain there. They put up so many bricks in the wall that they can't even see the person who shares their life. What has changed in the relationship? Only the brick wall—his chosen way of coping with pain. He has chosen the world's way of dealing with it. Isolation's answer to thorns is just to cut them off. Unfortunately, the isolated cut themselves off as well.

• God's Way—Facing Pain with New Eyes

And then there is God's way, which neither insulates or isolates us from grief's pain.

God's first way of dealing with pain is to examine the pain head-on. That's just the opposite of isolating and insulating.

As I was training to be a chaplain, I did a rotation in the emergency room of one of Sacramento's hospitals. Every person who came in there said, "Take away my pain!" Good emergency room doctors don't load you up right away with pain medicines; they

SELF-CHECK

• How have you insulated yourself?

_____

• How have you isolated yourself?

_____

want you to experience the pain to its fullest so they can see the intensity and damage of the problem. By measuring the level of your pain, they can diagnose your illness and prescribe the proper medication. But if doctors are wise enough to know what pain's positive effects are for us, how much more must God know?

We can walk around with a Superman mentality: "Me feel pain? Impossible!" We also stifle pain with a martyr mentality: "I feel pain, but I will hide it from everyone forever, since venting my pain might hurt others." God's way, however, is to acknowledge how we feel. Open yourself up to the pain of your loss. Face it. Stop stuffing it. Stop venting it. Stop isolating or insulating yourself. Instead, admit it: "Lord, I'm hurting right now. This person has hurt me. This situation has caused me pain."

God knows, and he's willing and able. The problem isn't God's ability or his availability; the problem is our wrong thinking. We go to God the same way we go to that emergency room: "I want this fixed, and I want it fixed yesterday! I didn't even want to experience this. Don't teach me anything, just take the pain away. I don't care how you do it, just do it."

I can hear you now: _What do you mean, accept pain? God can't want that! I'm not accepting pain!_ But if I were to tell you that by accepting your pain, you'd be guaranteed to feel better, could you do it?

Let's take out our biblical resource tool and read the quote from Paul's letter to the

SELF-CHECK

- Are you acting like Superman or Wonder Woman? In what ways have you been dealing with the pain of your loss as if you were a man or woman of steel?

_____

What to do: Let yourself be fully human. How can you do that?

_____

Romans (5:3-5). In your own words, describe the apostle Paul's thought in the lines below:

_____

_____

This is a message that has been lost in the church today. "Oh, I want the glory of God. I want the power of God. But that suffering stuff, that isn't for us today." In America we are in danger of only limiting ourselves to half the gospel. We like all the good parts but ignore this part. Paul wrote this to the church. He said we should rejoice in the sufferings because we know that suffering produces perseverance. He says that perseverance builds character, and character, hope.

Many people have told me that they owe their faith to the fact that in the midst of the horrible pain of their loss, they encountered the truth of this verse. That's the power of pain in our lives: to transform us, to get our attention, to refocus our perspective, to transform our lives and draw us back to the God who created us.

What happens when you stop running from your pain? What happens when you stop isolating and insulating and start looking straight at the pain? There will be a moment when you can do this. You will be truthful with God, saying, "I'm hurting right now, and I need your help." That will be your turning point.

Then your prayer is no longer, "Lord, take away my pain." Your prayer becomes, "Lord, help me to understand. Help me understand the principles that my loss can teach me."

Don't get me wrong. I'm not advocating that you suffer needlessly. The pain we're discussing is the emotional pain that has come from your loss. God has a purpose in this process of pain. God wants to bring about great things through the losses in your life if you will just let him.

If you are quick to medicate, if you are quick to deny, if you are quick to suppress, and if you live a life outside of reality, you may miss one of the turning points built in to us and miss the

> We also rejoice in our sufferings, because we know that suffering produces perseverance; perseverance, character; and character, hope. And hope does not disappoint us, because God has poured out his love into our hearts by the Holy Spirit, whom he has given us.
>
> *Romans 5:3-5*

blessing waiting there. You rob God of the privilege of the reward. He wants to turn your pain into a blessing.

How do we keep handling our pain God's way and not the human way? We do it by nurturing the proper perspective of our pain and its role in our spiritual growth. What greater person can we look at than Jesus, who suffered pain and had to deal with it and acknowledge it and accept it. In the midst of your pain, consider Christ, the "Rose of Sharon." How did he cope with the thorns? How did he endure the cross? How did Jesus endure the beatings? The betrayals? The bruising, the crown of thorns placed upon his head, the nails that were put into his hands and feet? How did Jesus endure? He endured the pain of the cross, the book of Hebrews says, because he saw the joy that was set before him. He could see the joy, the finished product (12:2-3). He didn't say that through pain and suffering all of a sudden you would have character. He said in your endurance of the pain and suffering he will build character. We can only do that by modeling what Christ did. He was the ultimate model. He endured.

God has joy for you on the other side of your pain if you are willing to endure. Not mask. Not hide. Not insulate. Not isolate. Not avoid. But acknowledge and let God build endurance and character in your life. God has a plan of joy on the other side. Focus on the joy set before you. When you resist insulating yourself, you open your heart to God, and he will draw near. Instead of running from the pain, you can run to God. Instead of being mad at God about having the pain, you can make the important requests:

> "Let us fix our eyes on Jesus, the author and perfecter of our faith, who for the joy set before him endured the cross."
>
> Hebrews 12:2

God, I want to be convinced that there is a purpose for this.

God, I want to be convinced that you love me.

God, what is the lesson in my life?

When you come to that place, your body becomes healthy, your mind becomes healthy, your emotions become healthy, your spirit becomes healthy. And you begin to understand that peace that passes all understanding that is talked about so much during loss, because you are looking at your pain through your new lenses. You're seeing it from a God's-eye view. No longer are you fighting God about this pain. You are open to the pathway through it to something better—someone better: you.

> In all these things we are more than conquerors through him who loved us. For I am convinced that neither death nor life...
> nor anything else in all creation, will be able to separate us from the love of God that is in Christ Jesus our Lord.
>
> Romans 8:37-39

PAUSE TO REFLECT

God wants to bring about great things through your life crisis. Here, in the privacy of your workbook, answer these questions:

• Which of these prayers have you prayed? Underline any or all:

Lord, take away my pain.
God, why did you allow this?
God, where are you?
God, I am so mad at you, so mad at everything for this loss!

• Which one of these prayers might you be able to pray? Underline whatever you can:

Lord, help me to understand.
God, help me to recognize the principles that you are teaching me.
God, help me to see things from your God's-eye view.

Your own prayer: _____

_____

_____

_____

Work It Out

1. Your heart is breaking. The pain is real, suffocating. You can hardly face it. How can you help yourself take this major leap onto the road to recovery? List two ideas:

_____

_____

2. Think hard. What might be one lesson you could learn from your pain?

_____

_____

3. What does the term "the peace that passes all understanding" mean to you?

_____

_____

_____

Grief Recovery Journal

Date _____

Dear _____ :

This is how I feel right now:

_____

_____

_____

_____

_____

_____

_____

_____

_____

_____

_____

This is what I've discovered today:

_____

_____

_____

_____

_____

_____

_____

_____

_____

_____

This is what I still question today:

_____

_____

_____

_____

_____

_____

_____

_____

_____

_____

_____

Extra space to finish your thoughts, if needed:

_____

_____

_____

_____

_____

_____

_____

_____

_____

_____

For additional encouragement, listen to Number 10 on the *Grief Recovery Workbook CD*

Chapter 10

Anger: *But I'm So Mad!*

Dan Elledge was a young minister in a small town north of San Francisco. He decided he wanted to pastor a church, so he started one. Soon, he'd found a building which was a former adult movie theatre and turned it into a church which quickly thrived.

On a Wednesday afternoon, when he was alone in the church, two gunmen came in to rob the church. Dan's office was on the third story of the building, and when he went to investigate, he interrupted them. They opened fire, shooting him ten times. This magnificent man of God died on the outside steps of the church. A county animal control officer was driving by at the time and saw Dan lying across the steps and the two men rushing away. He began to follow them, and they were soon caught. The two turned out to be illegal aliens who were behind a series of unsolved church robberies. This had been the first that also included a murder.

Dan was gone, leaving behind a pregnant wife, a handsome son, and a church full of mourners. According to all we believe as Christians, he was in a better place. But that didn't stop the grief felt by those he left behind, especially the 150 members of his church—and the anger that came along with it. These Christian people were still very angry. They were angry with Dan: Why couldn't he have just left it alone? Why did he have to chase them? They were angry with the criminals, as well as the entire culture that produced them: How dare they come to our country and rob churches! And ultimately, they were mad at the justice system for the length of time it took to finally punish the murderers. But they were angry, most of all, at God: How could you take our leader?

Anger is, perhaps, the strongest of the major emotions related to the grief process. It certainly feels like the strongest, and it's the one most applicable to all forms of grief. Your anger can go so many ways:

> You can feel anger toward yourself for getting sick.
> You can feel anger toward God for not healing your illness.
> You can feel anger toward your loved one for dying.
> You can feel anger toward your loved ones who don't understand.
> You can feel anger toward the mortician for his lack of compassion.
> You can feel anger toward everyone else in the world who is happy when you're not.

Your anger can change from day to day, year to year, but it's still anger. And it can soon turn into blame. People blame themselves, but that's usually short-term. People blame others, but we are able to forgive others quicker than seemingly possible. But blaming God—that's the one that lingers. This is probably true for many reasons, but perhaps one of the most pervasive is, it seems to be forbidden and therefore goes unexpressed the longest, causing more pain and more damage. But God's not afraid of that anger. Coping with even the most unthinkable feelings is a must for your healthy grief process. And how to do that, how even to approach your anger at God, is what this chapter is going to help you discover. You are never going to have inner peace until you have discovered your way through your anger at God, others, and yourself.

Anger is an emotion which can be directed or destructive, depending on whether it is managed or mismanaged. It is always a formidable barrier to harmonious relationships and inner peace. To handle your anger, you need to understand it. Let's look at its symptoms, its sources, its stages, and then at strategies to acknowledge and ultimately overcome it.

SYMPTOMS OF ANGER

One night, I was watching a *Dateline* story on TV about what's wrong with America. The reporter said something I knew was incredibly true: We've become this nation of "indiscriminate expressers." Our pendulum has swung from one side, where we were taught to be suppressors—where we didn't talk about things, where we hid things to our detriment—to the other side, where anything and everything goes. For a long time now in most therapeutic circles, we have taught people to "vent" their anger. Mental health is found when you express it, get it out, do whatever you have to do to release the negative energy in a positive way so you can let go.

As with most things, there is an element of truth in that thinking, but as with most things, a good thing can become a bad thing when taken to extremes. And when that happens, we will have lost what little control we may have had, which can cause destructive consequences. If we are letting anger control our lives and our actions and our reactions, then we're certainly not letting God control our lives.

"Well, then," you ask, "how, in my frustration and anxiety and grief, do I *not* feel angry?" A certain amount of anger is as natural as all the other emotions you are feeling. So the question to ask is: "How do I know if I have an anger problem?"

Overt Anger

Anger expression is either overt or covert. We express our anger overtly by yelling, screaming, and the more obvious signs of expressing ourselves verbally and physically. We explode into a rage, and explosions are rarely controlled. Maybe you beat up on pillows, use bad language, or write that hateful letter. A rising phenomena on our freeways is something called "road rage," a term coined for random violence and outbursts of anger, set off by the pressures of traffic. Whether you've experienced such an explosion of emotion, or whether you've been a witness or target of it, you know that it is not a pleasant experience. Still, it happens from time to time in all our lives.

Sometimes when all our overt expression doesn't quite work, we might over-exercise. Sound familiar? At first, some might be envious and even admiring of such an ambitious, "health-conscious" person. Then something seems a little off, a little over the top. Your sense is probably correct. Exercising compulsively is another way people vent their suppressed anger.

Covert Anger

We express anger covertly by internalizing our feelings. We pretend not to be angry. Most people over sixty years old use this style of anger management, since they grew up during America's "suppressive" years, when we were taught to control our emotions by denying them: "Just be quiet. If you don't talk about it, it isn't really there. Whatever you do, don't express it in public."

Of course, people who are in denial of anger can suddenly surprise themselves, as well as everyone near them, by flying into a rage. "Whoa, where did that come from?" is the usual response. Anger, soon or later, will come out. Covert anger management, therefore, only works for a certain amount of time. Eventually, covert anger will become overt anger. That's probably the way I manage my anger far too much. I'm one of those people who fools myself into believing I'm not really angry. Then I explode, and I can't take it back. That may sound like I have an anger problem. But it's not really an anger problem; it's a problem of not dealing with anger on a regular basis.

"Sweeping it under the rug" is a figure of speech familiar to everyone. It's used to describe this very act of ignoring something important in hopes of it disappearing. But I see the reality of the image every week at my house. We choose one day a week to clean the house. In our kitchen area, we have these throw rugs. And every week, I am amazed at how much food I find under them. I never see anybody pick up the rugs and shove food under there. But every single week, when I pick up those rugs, I find reminders of every meal we had. And that reminds me how it is with life. We don't think our anger is a problem if we aren't turning red and stomping and shouting. But suppressed anger doesn't go away. Each day you are sweeping that little bit of anger dust under the carpet. And one day you find yourself flat on your face, having tripped over that big dirt mound you've created.

But, you're probably thinking, *if I only explode once every six months or so, surely that can't be so bad.* A volcano only blows up once every thousand years or so, yet it causes a lot of destruction when it does. Explosions are never good for anyone, no matter how rare or how common they are. But denial is not healthy either. Nudging those feelings out of sight doesn't mean they've vanished.

Covertly, we internalize it or deny it; overtly, we express it or vent it. And neither approach works.

PAUSE TO REFLECT

- Why are you angry?

_____

_____

_____

- Who or what is making you the most angry?

_____

_____

_____

- How are you currently expressing your anger?

_____

_____

_____

SOURCES OF ANGER

To begin working on dealing with your anger, we need to figure out its sources. What specifically can create our anger? To be able to manage it, we need to know the answer to that question. There are three sources that I've noticed create anger in most crisis situations.

1. Injustice

One of the first things that makes us angry is sensing an injustice around us or having an injustice happen to us. In fact, this is such a prevalent feeling in grief recovery that we began our workbook with the verbalization of this feeling: *It isn't fair!*

I often compare that feeling to a light bulb that's about to go out. Often light bulbs flicker before they burn out. They send us an indication that something is wrong. The injustice thought usually precedes anger. It normally comes before the explosion, before the venting, before the denial.

So when you hear yourself talking about the unfairness of life, that should be an indication to you that something is wrong. The light is about to go out (you'll attempt to stifle the anger), or an explosion is about to happen (you'll let the anger express itself).

2. Humiliation and Frustration

Another anger source is the feeling of humiliation, followed quickly by frustration:

How dare they do that!
Do you know what they did to me?
I'm not taking this anymore!
I just can't do this anymore!

Hear the anger, the hostility? See the light bulb flickering before the burnout? Or think of the image I described earlier to explain the importance of our emotions. Think of that flashing dashboard light. You sense an injustice, then you feel the humiliation, and that creates your frustration, and suddenly:

I just can't do this anymore!

My youngest daughter, when she was small, was a good example of this type of anger expression. When she got angry, it was because she was frustrated. She couldn't tie her shoes or button her shirt like her older sister and brother did, and she would get so frustrated, she'd just sit down, not wanting to be touched or moved. We all know that feeling.

3. Other Angry People

A third source of anger is learned behavior from other people. Their expression of anger is infectious.

This is the only way I know how to respond.
I have a right to respond this way.
That's how my parents expressed their emotions.

When we're around "expressers," or those who vent, we pick up those behaviors ourselves. We've learned from television, from parents, from schoolteachers, from friends. To say, "This is just the way I am," or "This is how I respond to situations," is a cop-out. What you are really saying is, "I don't want to change."

The good news is, you can unlearn these behaviors and you can learn godly behavior if you decide to do so. If your purpose is to grow in your spiritual life and maturity, then you can give up your old ways and learn new ones.

By the way, be aware of the focus of your anger as well. Unfortunately, the object of your anger is not always the source of your anger. And this can be especially true when you are going through the grieving process. "Don't take it out on me" is a common phrase heard by any anger expresser with close relationships. We tend to express our anger where we feel safe. So if we are mad at our boss, or God, or our extended family members, we may take it out on our spouse, our kids, or even our pets. If this sounds familiar, it's because you think you are controlling your frustrations, but you bring them home with you, and the slightest thing causes an explosion.

> "Bad company corrupts good character."
>
> *1 Corinthians 15:33*

To understand the stages of anger will also help you manage your anger. Let's list how your anger can progress to a problem level.

STAGES OF ANGER

The first stage of anger is *irritation*: "That really bothers me."

The second stage is *indignation*: "I cannot believe this is happening to me. This isn't right. It's not fair!"

The third stage is *vengeance*: "She's going to pay for what she did!"

The fourth stage is *rage*: "He got what he deserved." "I have every right to..."

And then all of these can culminate in a stage of anger that can often create even more tragedy—*fury*: "I don't know what happened. I just blew up."

We've all heard stories of people opening fire in post offices—"going postal" is what it's come to be called—or walking into a police department and blankly surrendering after a tragic event fueled by anger-induced fury. I've actually been called in to work with people who have killed their spouse or other close loved ones. As we help this person through the funeral or to cope with prison, they will often say, "I don't even remember the gun, the shooting, or anything about it." The rage turned to psychotic fury and their behavior surprised even them. Their fury spent, such people rarely show emotion while describing the crime. They have been totally deranged by their anger.

Anger left unchecked doesn't go away. It only grows into something either destructive to yourself or to others—or both. Sometimes you may have to give yourself permission to acknowledge your anger. Especially those who have been taught that anger is un-Christian. During many disasters, I often hear this misconception about anger expressed.

A firefighter I met during my work in New York City after the September 11 World Trade Center attack had that kind of anger, and he didn't know what to do with it. I met him one rainy, messy night in October at Ground Zero, during a shift spent combing through pieces in a stairwell. It was the sixth or seventh rain since the attack. Along with a team of firefighters and Emergency Service Unit members, I was on my hands and knees digging with my shovel for remains. On my hard-hat was the chaplain's symbol of a cross, which signaled to any of the workers that I was there for them anytime they needed to talk. During a pause in which we had to stand back for a heavy machine to cut away a section of the pile, a big, burly African-American police officer put a hand on something in his pants pocket. He fingered it a moment then pulled it out. It was one of the little Gideon Bibles. And when he spoke to me, it was through a jaw set as hard as stone.

"I know the Good Book says I'm supposed to forgive, to turn the other cheek, but I'm sorry, I just can't do that. I'm too angry. I don't know what to do, I'm so mad."

"Well, I'm standing here, and I'm mad too," I said. "Just stop for a minute and look around. Look at this mess! You're mad, I'm mad, God's mad!"

He squinted hard at me. "Are you saying that *God* is angry?"

"You bet. How could the Creator of the universe not disapprove of this? You better believe there's a place for righteous anger." I waved at the enormity of where we were standing, at the evilness of it all. "What do you think God is thinking right now? Here, God gave us freedom to make our own choices, and someone used it to fly planes into buildings and kill innocent people. If you ask me, I think God is very angry we would use our freedom to do something so horrible." I stopped to wipe the rain off my face. "You want to know something? You've shed a few tears over all this, right?"

"Right."

"Me too. Well, all this rain feels to me like God's tears crying over this place. I can't get that image out of my head. I'm crying, you're crying, God's crying. You know?"

"So are you saying that God is okay with me being angry?" he said, still finding it hard to believe.

"Listen," I answered, "the fact that you're asking about being close to God is enough, but your being here, angry or not, says it all. You just have to know how to handle it." My new friend's misconception about God's reaction to his anger almost caused him to miss the relationship God wanted to have with him that night at Ground Zero.

You now have a good grasp of anger's symptoms, sources, and stages. Let's chart a new course. To control your anger, you've tried the human way. First we were told to suppress it, and that didn't work. Then they told us to vent. That also didn't work. Either action goes against the way we were made. So if you can't vent it, express it, suppress it, or deny it to make it go away, what can you do?

I want to suggest another way, an old way you can make new for yourself—a response instead of a reaction, a choice instead of a reflex. Your anger can keep you separated from the only source that can give you peace. And that peace comes from a change in perspective through a God-given resource you already have. Let's talk about some strategies for dealing with the anger of your loss.

SELF-CHECK

- What is your anger temperature? In which stage of anger do you find yourself? Circle one of the following:

Irritable   Indignant   Vengeful   Wrathful   Furious

STRATEGIES FOR DEALING WITH ANGER

We have been talking about your possible anger with God, as well as recounting other grieving people's struggle with it in grief recovery. We want to know how a loving God could allow such pain and suffering. Before we can deal with strategies of healthy anger management, let's face these feelings and discuss them openly.

During my months of work at Ground Zero after the World Trade Center terrorist attack, the pervading question I was asked by people on the subway, at the site of the attacks, on the street, was this one: *Where was God? How could he let this happen? Does God care at all?*

It's also what the young murdered pastor's congregation wanted to know. It was what the two grieving mothers who lost their sons to random violence wanted to know. It's at the heart of the age-old question asked in the aftermath of every atrocity of history. And it's what you want to know about your own tragedy. Where was God?

A New York City detective named Beth asked that question. I met her as I was finishing my night shift rotation at Ground Zero. The sun had just come up, and I saw her leaning on a piece of construction equipment. She was wearing jeans and a detective's badge, but I still thought her being there at that time of day was odd. It had been a cold and rainy night. The sunlight had just come through the buildings. She was soaking it in, sitting all by herself. I introduced myself and asked her where she had been during the attacks.

"Right here," she said, "working in a triage area we'd set up. There were firefighters here with us, and we were all helping people who'd been hurt when the planes crashed into the towers." She paused, looking past me. "Until the building came down."

The force of the implosion blew her thirty yards, into a revolving door, along with two firemen who had instinctively covered her with their own bodies an instant before the collapse. Everyone else near her in the triage area, she told me, was somewhere under the fallen building. She had come every day since the attack, always to the same spot, always at the same time, trying to make sense of the senseless. "Why did I live? Why did God let this happen?" she asked.

In the aftermath of tragedy, most questions about God are really about dealing with loss, I've learned. The reality of a deadly catastrophe seems to imply that God hid his face, ran away, left the scene—the presumption being that the absence of God allowed the tragedy to happen: If God is God, where was he? If God was here, then how could this happen? This was the biggest spiritual obstacle people expressed after September 11. To feel a sense of God in joyous moments of life seems natural. But we cannot imagine why or how a loving God could be present during suffering of any kind. Yet how can we explain the stories told of God's presence amid such atrocities as the Jewish Holocaust during World War II? And how do we explain the stories that survivors of September 11 have told—of small choices or still, small voices keeping them home, making them late to work, or leading to a stairwell in the dark?

"Why did God do this?" Beth had asked me that morning.

I explained what I believed—that such evil was against the nature of a creator whom I call my "heavenly Father."

"Then why did God allow it?" If God could have stopped it and didn't, this survivor had to believe that something was wrong with us or something was wrong with God.

Beth and I, sitting there in the morning sun, explored the very basics of the Christian faith and its mystery—our free will, God's sovereignty, God's grace. Yet despite all the theological talk, she still could not get past the deaths that had occurred so near her. It was the memory that had her locked tight. "But those people standing right beside me," she said. "What about them?"

Throughout all I've seen in this work, all the things I've heard, and all the things I trust, there is one belief I rest in. It is what allows me to keep doing this work, no matter how grim it becomes. And that belief, I realized, was what would give Beth the comfort she needed.

I told her where I believed God was during the disaster.

"Let's say you're right and that God did allow this to happen," I began. "To have such influence, that would mean God is all-powerful, right?"

"Yes," she agreed.

"Then, in the time the buildings were hit and then collapsed, can you believe that God was also powerful enough to help every single one of the people who died?"

At that, she paused. She was silent for a long moment, then tears came to her eyes. "You mean if God could have helped them to live, then he could have helped them to die?"

"God could have wrapped his arms around every single one," I said, "and helped them go into eternity. Even those who may have lived on the pile for several days before dying could have known God's presence right there in the ruins with them."

She gazed back at the spot where the ones around her had died, and so did I.

The struggle still existed, I admitted to her. We still had a choice: we could believe that a God big enough to allow such a disaster was also big enough to help everyone affected, or we could believe that God wasn't big enough or perhaps didn't care. "Believing one will bring you peace; the other will bring you hopelessness," I added. "But anybody who would come back here for fourteen days straight already knows the answer."

My answer to you would be the same that I offered Beth. God was there. God is here. But you can answer that question for yourself. These strategies will be an attempt to gain God's perspective, his God's-eye view, which changes everything—and I do mean everything.

You can think in a worldly way, in an ungodly way. You can think about the get-even road, or you can try lining up your thinking with God's thinking. If you do, you can find your whole mind transformed with each reminder. All of a sudden you find your blood pressure going down and your ability to think returns. And you find the energy to move to the next step.

You have experienced a tragedy, a horrible injustice. You can express it overtly or covertly, but if you also use God's biblical resource, you now have a choice. This strategy won't be a quick fix. You long for the fast-food solution lane, a drive-through answer. This way is a long sit-down dinner at God's dining table with each course building on another, from soup to nuts. But it will be far worth it. Ready?

HANDLING ANGER

There are three ways to handle your anger from God's view: Think biblically, speak biblically, and act biblically.

Think Biblically

Thinking biblically doesn't mean remembering rules and regulations, but *remembering promises*. First, you should remember who God is and his promises to care for you. Why consider those promises first? To remind you how precious you are to God, and why God has always been precious to you. And the way you can do that is to, first, remember the biblical promises that God made to all of us—to you.

Psalm 23 is universally beloved, and for good reason. David wrote it to express the peace that comes from God's presence during hard times, even through the threat of death. Our human way of thinking sees death as the worst thing that can happen to us: Our life is over, our relationship with our children is interrupted, and it's the end of everything we have ever known. That grand old psalm, though, suggests that we don't even have to fear death. We don't have to think of it as an injustice because God is right there with us.

What is God's perspective about death?

The struggle we humans have with the issue of death comes from being unable to see death as God must see it. A God-perspective of death is not one we humans easily embrace—that death is a part of life, even when it is at the hands of other human beings. I recall reading a statistic during that time which stated that seven thousand Americans die each day. Death is something we all will face, but to God, death isn't a terrible thing. In the Christian tradition, it's actually a graduation. According to my faith system, it is a continuance of life because of faith in Christ, a moving into God's presence with all the joy that

> Even though I walk through the valley of the shadow of death, I will fear no evil, for you are with me.
>
> *Psalm 23:4*

promises. Or, as I've expressed the thought at many memorial services, death is not a period, but a comma. God's perspective is, death isn't the worst thing, it's the best thing.

If there's a message from God through crisis, even amid our own anger at him, it has to be that this life isn't everything. There's a whole life beyond this life, a whole existence beyond this planet. This isn't our home. The "peace that passes understanding" that we all pray to have in the middle of sorrow starts with having that proper perspective about death.

So when we're talking about thinking biblically, we're first talking about taking God at his word. He promised to care for us and he promised to never leave us. Thinking biblically begins with believing God's promises.

The second way to think biblically is to actually dwell upon how God has forgiven us.

Thinking about how the mercy of God has been demonstrated to you leads you to realize that you can do the same to others. Part of your ability to move past your anger and to process it in a biblical way is to think about how you've been forgiven. Forgive as the Lord forgave you.

This may be your first hard step forward. *No way I can do that.* That's what you're thinking, isn't it? Be patient with yourself, but don't allow your anger to blind you to this potent idea. Thinking of being forgiven pushes your narrow perspective larger. It takes your anger and puts it into proper, God's-eye view-perspective. When you can say, "God, you had every right, but yet you forgave me," then you open yourself up to the future possibility of allowing forgiveness to seep into your own anger.

"Forgive as the Lord forgave you." There is no such thing as selective grace. This teaching says that you're in or you're out. We can't be selective of whom we are going to show mercy to when it comes to our anger.

But I bet I know something that may be even harder than forgiving those who've hurt you. How about forgiving yourself? Have you considered that you also need to stop directing that anger inward? If God can forgive you, why can't you forgive yourself? For some people, this may be the hardest type of forgiveness.

There is one more way to help yourself think biblically. I express it this way: I take every thought "captive to the obedience of Christ." In other words, take the thought captive and funnel it through what

> Be kind and compassionate to one another, forgiving each other, just as in Christ God forgave you.
>
> *Ephesians 4:32*

SELF-CHECK

- Are you angry at God?

_____

- Are you giving yourself permission to tell God how you feel?

_____

you know of Christ's example. When those angry thoughts come in, what do you do with them? In light of God's Word, what should your response be?

Paul told the Philippians how to deal with this, and in so doing, told us as well. If I set my mind on whatever is admirable, whatever is excellent, whatever is praiseworthy, I'll be okay. That's another way of saying, we are what we think. What becomes life to our bones becomes life to our soul. Don't think you can do it? Here is what Paul would say to that thought: "I can do everything through [Christ] who gives me strength" (Philippians 4:13).

> Bear with each other and forgive whatever grievances you may have against one another. Forgive as the Lord forgave you.
>
> *Colossians 3:13*

Speak Biblically

The first way that we speak biblically is to *speak slowly*, that is, to be slow to speak. Biblical speaking isn't just spouting off. Instead of thinking through what we're saying, anger makes us want to just speak out and throw the words out there, ultimately having to follow them up with an apology.

Put another way: If you haven't prayed about it, then don't say it. Here's how this

PAUSE TO REFLECT

Can you keep your thoughts under control? Does it sound impossible? When the stages of anger come rushing through you, can you take the thought captive and filter it through what you know of Christ's example?

Try it. Look up these four scriptures. Funnel your anger through them, then summarize their wisdom below for a new anger-management strategy to fit your need:

Ephesians 4:32
Colossians 3:13
Philippians 4:8
Colossians 3:2

_____

_____

_____

_____

_____

_____

_____

_____

_____

strategy works: Before you say a word to anyone, pray that God will give you guidance. Force yourself to ask, "Should I say this?" Let it go through the mind of God first—from God to you.

I believe that when I'm angry, the Lord is trying to tell *me* something. The lesson in slowing down is that we learn the all-important habit of first asking: *God, what are you saying to me?* For some people going through the grieving process, speaking biblically or, for that matter, using any of these strategies, might require getting another kind of anger acknowledged first. We have to acknowledge that we have this overwhelming anger in order to be free of it.

Believe it or not, admitting your anger is truly freeing: Just say, "Hey, I'm feeling angry," to somebody or to God, and feel the release. Then you can let it go.

I keep thinking of David's plea in Psalm 51:12, "Restore to me the joy of your salvation." Who among us hasn't felt that way when we've found ourselves grieving? Speaking biblically is how you can make your way back to that joy.

> Whatever is true, whatever is noble, whatever is right, whatever is pure, whatever is lovely, whatever is admirable—if anything is excellent or praiseworthy, think about such things.
>
> *Philippians 4:8*

We also speak biblically by using *words of encouragement.* God encourages us all the time with his Word, and we need to encourage one another. Neither venting nor suppressing works, remember? So acting as if you are doing fine must stop. Instead, encourage others and allow others to encourage you. We all need to be more transparent with one another. It helps us to grow and it helps us to be accountable with one another.

So think biblically about your anger before you express it, before you suppress it, before you deny it. Then speak biblically, and you will be able to move on to the next strategy—acting biblically.

Acting Biblically

At a difficult time in my own life, I decided that God wanted me to try something new. From that point on, with every single decision I made, from what to eat to where to go,

PAUSE TO REFLECT

Are you able to speak biblically? Plug in these two scriptures in light of your loss. Summarize and synthesize them into your new anger-management strategy:

2 Corinthians 2:6-8
Ephesians 4:30

_____

_____

_____

_____

_____

I was to just stop and listen. After I listened, I should wait. After I waited, I was to obey. Stop. Listen. Wait. Obey. Those four words, I came to understand, were the ones by which God wanted me to live my life. The effect was a life-changing one: I was always wondering what God thought about the matter. And that small opening in my thinking turned my perspective inside out.

Stop, listen, wait, obey—four words that truly changed my life.

Acting biblically comes easier after we have accepted the fact of God's scriptural resource. It's been guiding people through the tough times of their lives for centuries. Once we start thinking bib-

> A gentle answer turns away wrath, but a harsh word stirs up anger.
>
> *Proverbs 15:1*

lically, we find it easier to speak biblically, and even easier to act biblically. And that will be needed when you come to our next chapter's topic—forgiveness. But there can't be any discussion about forgiveness until you deal with your anger.

> "Everyone should be quick to listen, slow to speak and slow to become angry, for man's anger does not bring about the righteous life that God desires."
>
> *James 1:19–20*

Try these three ways of "acting biblically" to help move you over the anger obstacle on your recovery road journey. Discipline yourself to identify the anger signals and act differently when anger hits by acting biblically.

• *Your can of worms*: Ask yourself what you're mad about. What are your anger signals? You may be afraid to open up that can of worms because of what might come out. But you have to go there; you have to identify and then acknowledge the anger at its source. That's where healing starts.

• *Scripture in your head*: Another way to act differently is to memorize Scripture. A Bible isn't going to help you when you're angry. No one says, "I'm angry! Where's my Bible?" The only Scripture that is going to help you when you're mad is the kind that's already hid in your heart.

• *Praying for whom?* Acting biblically can also be energized by prayer—and not just prayer for yourself. Try praying for those whom you need to forgive or those who have

SELF-CHECK

• The Scriptures demand we be doers of God's Word and not just hearers (James 1:22). While in your grief process, how are you able to "do" and not just "listen"?

> Do not merely listen to
> the word, and so
> deceive yourselves.
> Do what it says.
>
> *James 1:22*

been a source of anger. That's what is going to bring the heart of God to you.

You've learned the sources of your anger, the stages of your anger, and new, God-filled strategies for diffusing your anger. God's way is to think biblically, to speak biblically, and then to act biblically. When we do that, we can regain our joy and peace, which is the destination of our grief process.

With your new management strategies for anger, you now have a choice whether anger controls you or you control it.

Work It Out

1. What is the source of your anger? What are you really mad about? Can you identify it now? This is where the healing starts:

   _____

   _____

2. What verses for memorization would work best for your personal "biblical" strategy? List them below and act on them. Remember, the only scriptures that are going to help you are the ones already in your head:

   _____   _____

   _____   _____

   _____   _____

3. Try the most novel biblically based anger management of all: Pray for those you need to forgive or those who have been a source of anger. Who will you pray for?

   _____

Explain why you can or cannot do this yet in your journal pages that follow.

PAUSE TO REFLECT

If you've found yourself angry at anyone or anything in relation to your loss, get it off your chest in a biblical way. In the following space (or on a separate piece of paper), write a letter to that person expressing your innermost feelings. No one needs to ever see your letter, so be totally honest.

Dear _____,

I am so angry at you because …

Sincerely,

Grief Recovery Journal

Date _____

Dear _____ :

This is how I feel right now:

_____

_____

_____

_____

_____

_____

_____

_____

_____

_____

This is what I've discovered today:

_____

_____

_____

_____

_____

_____

_____

_____

_____

_____

This is what I still question today:

_____

_____

_____

_____

_____

_____

_____

_____

_____

Extra space to finish your thoughts, if needed:

_____

_____

_____

_____

_____

_____

_____

_____

_____

_____

For additional encouragement, listen to
Number 11 on the *Grief Recovery Workbook CD*

Chapter 11

The Crossroad of Grief:
I Can Never Forgive

It happened outside Union Square subway station a few months after the World Trade Center attack. I went to see how people were coping, having heard that ordinary people were coming to this place to share their pain about the event in an open-air dialogue. I went expecting to hear their thoughts and feelings, but what I found was raw emotion. A young woman suddenly yelled in my direction: "I hate you and what you stand for! I hate all religions! They're the reason that all these people died!"

Behind the young woman stood an older woman, quiet, nervous, and embarrassed. The pair were obviously mother and daughter. The mother was a Christian, I learned, but she could only stand by as her daughter vented her frustrations on the collar around my neck and the cross on my uniform for all the ills of religious fanaticism. I guessed that I had just become a part of an old issue between the pair. For all I knew, I was the latest in a long line of chaplains, pastors, and priests she had confronted since September 11.

But I only had a short time to respond, I knew. My task at a national disaster was not to strike up a street debate, but to nudge stalled thinking into gear once more—to offer something that might give comfort in a new way while helping her move past her anger. No argument, even one she won, was going to make her feel better that day.

So I chose to look at her need, and what I saw seemed to include her mother. "I understand your frustration," I said. "The answers we all need may be impossible to know right now. Even I'm confused by all of this." She softened her gaze as if to say, "I'm sorry for forgetting that you, too, are human." I then asked her about what seemed to be more important than my faith or hers. "You love your mom, right?"

She glanced at her mother, "Yes."

"How long would be enough to be able to be with her? Twenty years?"

"I suppose."

"How about fifty years?"

"Yes, that'd be great."

"How about if it could be forever?"

She paused. "You're talking about heaven, aren't you?"

"It's one of the good things about your mom's faith: life after death—no matter how death comes or when," I answered. "If you're right about all religions, there's nothing ahead to hold on to. But if your mother's faith in Christ is right, then you'll always be with her. There's not a whole lot more to the choice, really."

The young woman, surprised at the direction the conversation had taken, said nothing. A rose vendor approached us. Normally, I would never have bought one, but that day I did.

"Here, this is for you." I held it out to the young woman.

She took it, her eyes softening and reddening a bit. "I'll place it on the memorial." She took a step toward one of the makeshift memorials that dotted the subway station entrance, one of hundreds in the area.

"No, no," I said. "That's for you. Press it in a book, and years from now you'll find it, and you and your mom will remember this night."

I left mother and daughter to their thoughts as I descended into the subway station. Most of my chats during my months working at Ground Zero were like that, some shorter, some longer.

> "In your anger do not sin":
> Do not let the sun go down
> while you are still angry.
>
> *Ephesians 4:26*

Almost all of them were reflections of where each person was in the grief process over the disaster, how it had affected them personally, where they were stuck on their own road to recovery. For most New Yorkers, the concept of forgiveness would have been an impossible idea at the time, yet it would be a much-needed step toward any kind of future healing. It would not come quickly nor easily. During my sixty-eight days there, I didn't expect to see any such dramatic results from my efforts. The grief process is always a slow one.

But that day was different; I was offered a peek into one person's future. About twenty minutes after I'd left the two women and had gone into the subway system, I was still in there, reading a memorial wall. As I was reading the tribute to a port authority officer erected as a shrine outside his duty station, I felt a tap on my shoulder. It was the daughter. And she was suddenly giving me a big hug. "I just wanted to catch you, to tell you that, well, I still have lots of questions, but the answers don't seem as hard. Thank you."

As she rushed away, I don't mind telling you that I was suddenly the one with red eyes. What does it take to forgive? What kind of forgiveness does your grief process demand? How do you even begin the journey needed to get to the healing on the other side of the act of forgiveness?

Questions like these must be going through your mind as you start a chapter that deals with forgiveness. True forgiveness is so rare and so against our human nature that it seems downright unnatural. Forgiveness goes against everything that we've heard or learned in life. We are often told that the only way to feel better about our loss is to get even—or at the very least, to carry a grudge to our grave. We believe this so deeply in our society that forgiveness must become a willful decision. It becomes a choice to take the path less taken, a path that does not allow someone else's actions or some inexplicable event to dictate our attitude. It is recovery's crossroad. What path will you take?

ABSOLUTES OF FORGIVENESS

Forgiveness is important to your grief recovery for two very important reasons. First, forgiveness is essential to your health and well-being, and second, God, in his wisdom, tells us to forgive.

Forgiveness is essential to your health.

"C'mon," I hear you say. "Whether I forgive or not doesn't make any difference. My grudge is not really hurting anybody." But that's where you are wrong. It is hurting somebody: you. And that is what I want to show you in the next few pages.

Forgiveness isn't something we can do a little bit. It's not a graded act. It's pass/fail. You are either walking in the freedom of forgiveness, or you are walking bound up in your bitterness and anger. The one who is hurt the most by a lack of forgiveness will always be you. It hurts you emotionally, it hurts you physically, and it obviously hurts you spiritually. When you walk in unforgiveness, you leave yourself open to stumbling over the boulders of bitterness along the trail. It is easy to stumble when you are distracted.

Sometimes when I walk, it is very early and I find myself on the trail while it is still dark. It is at these times I am most apt to trip along the rocks that lie below the surface yet have an edge exposed. When you are in the middle of your loss, you may think you can live with its spiritual effects. But sooner or later, the unforgiveness will find another way to express itself, and you'll be tripped up along the way.

Again, forgiveness is an act of your will; it's a choice that you make. If you say, "I can't forgive," you are really saying, "I don't want to. I choose not to." Yet it is essential to your long-term physical, emotional, and spiritual well-being.

God asks you to forgive.

Second, you may not want to hear this one, but for any Christian, forgiveness is an absolute. We must forgive because God asked us to. God doesn't say, "If you'd like to forgive," or "If you feel like forgiving, please do so." Scripture says rather plainly that by the measure that we forgive, we will be forgiven. If we don't forgive, we won't be forgiven.

> "Forgive, and you will be forgiven....For with the measure you use, it will be measured to you."
>
> *Luke 6:37-38*

"But I can't do that," you may say. "I just can't forgive."

If you believe that, you're limiting God. God doesn't ask us to do something that he hasn't enabled or equipped us to do. He's asking us to trust him and try. God has our best interest in mind, because he knows the consequences of those boulders of bitterness.

Maybe the one you feel you need to forgive is God. That may be what is holding you back. You're wondering how you can even think such a thing, much less see it in print! God might hear it! But I'm sure you know that he knows. We discussed this situation in chapter 10 concerning anger. You are not the first person to be conflicted about God's role in your pain.

Maybe you wonder where God was when you lost your loved one, or when you were hurt so terribly by that accident or that illness or that trusted person. Maybe you are like the young woman in the New York subway station after 9/11. On whatever level you feel the pain of your argument with the God of the universe, you must consider how to get beyond the seemingly impregnable wall of such an unthinkable thought. You need to think the thought and then express it.

Recently I had the privilege of working with the people of Maryland after a series of sniper shootings which at the time had killed 10 people and injured three others in their region. The randomness of the violence had been felt by the entire community and had left many people paralyzed with fear. In addition to the fear, anxiety, and anger that surfaced in the face of these senseless murders, I found a greater problem among the people—boulders of bitterness. As the snipers were captured, the fear and anxiety immediately subsided. But the anger and bitterness towards these men remained, and could easily undermine people's healing for years to come.

Fortunately, many of the churches and a Christ-centered counseling center had the foresight to deal with the issue of unforgiveness. I am confident that the physical and emotional impact of the shootings within these communities will be greatly curtailed by the prayers of forgiveness being offered toward the perpetrators of these evil events.

But how can you pray for these evil men? How could they ever be forgiven? Remember, God's the one who asks this of us. He will be right there to help the people who suffer with the task of forgiveness. In fact, he's right here as you read the rest of this chapter, and he will help you through this pivotal point in your grief journey.

EFFECTS OF UNFORGIVENESS

First, let's consider specifically some of the things that happen when you can't forgive.

Being unforgiving affects all areas of your life. If you need to forgive someone in your business life, it affects your church life and your family life. Unforgiveness keeps you stuck, and stuck hard. You're trying to change the channel, but the same program is playing on and on. Not being able to forgive affects you in five different, dramatic ways. The following are the effects on our lives when we choose not to forgive.

Unforgiveness adds to your feelings of loneliness and isolation.

Who wants to feel more lonely and isolated? Yet that's what unforgiveness does. Loneliness just gets increasingly worse. While forgiveness eases the lonely feeling, unforgiveness just draws us more into ourselves as we nurture our hate and hurt. We end up insulating and isolating ourselves.

Unforgiveness allows anger to fester.

Think about your life. Think about that time when someone may have hurt you or didn't treat you properly. Think about your anger toward them and then say, "Okay, I have a choice. I can walk in the path of forgiveness, or I can stumble into the boulders of bitterness." Personally reflect upon this question: Did your anger toward that person ever go away? If not, how has your anger helped you since?

The latter is really a rhetorical question, of course. Anger really doesn't help us, and neither does unforgiveness. It allows anger to fester.

Unforgiveness causes physical and emotional distress.

Being unable to forgive will only add to your physical and emotional distress. Do you know what I have found as people have shared with me over the years? I've found that people will do really well with overcoming their guilt, and they will do really well in the area of anger and fear and pain and loneliness. But most people journeying through grief recovery get stuck in their grief right here: They just can't get past the personal obstacles they've placed in the way of forgiving.

Death penalty arguments aside, studies have shown that while public executions may offer a form of closure, they offer little in the way of pain relief for the survivors. Much of the time, survivors will make such comments as: "It was too easy." "He didn't show any remorse." "It wasn't enough. It will never be enough." "I thought it would help. It didn't."

Unforgiveness allows the physical impact of grief to linger longer, and it keeps us strapped into the emotional roller coaster. Is it any wonder that we feel so sick when we allow bitterness to remain in our lives?

The real issue becomes to move on with our grief. To resolve the issue personally—each survivor finding his or her own way.

Unforgiveness imprisons you in the past.

Unforgiveness connects you to the people who have hurt you. They continue to hurt you by the events to which you are still attached. Because you haven't forgiven, you inflict yourself with the pain over and over again, since you are still connected to them.

"Why should I let this person off the hook?" you may say. But it's not a matter of letting that person off the hook. Forgiveness lets *you* off the hook. Often, I can meet people who have gone through a traumatic event who talk about the event as though it happened yesterday. And yet it happened fifteen, even twenty years ago. They've been carrying this stuff around with them for a large part of their lives. I hear this too often with divorce. The spouses who caused the pain have gone on with their lives. They're often remarried, even have children. They have a wonderful life, while the wronged spouse is still imprisoned to the past.

> Cast all your anxiety on him because he cares for you.
>
> *1 Peter 5:7*

Sometimes your attitude and actions are so closely connected to being unforgiving that the unforgiveness dictates where you go and who you see. "I can't go to that coffee shop or that church or that store because I might run into the person I hate." So does that dictate your actions? Absolutely.

Unforgiveness yields the control of your life to the person who hurt you.

One of the hardest things about grief is that we no longer have control of our circumstances, and unforgiveness keeps that control even further from our grasp.

You cannot regain control of your life until you win your battle with forgiveness. Too much of your life has already been taken away from you by the loss. Every second you cannot forgive is another second that person has stolen from you.

Often, forgiveness in this country is just a foreign concept. It's almost seen as wimpy, when actually it's very noble. It's a difficult idea for Americans to grasp. We have been reared hearing about our "inalienable rights." The individual's rights in America are what we prize above all. The concept of forgiveness doesn't fit into that. Why? "Because I have a right to be mad. I have a right to be angry. I have a right to demand a pound of flesh. I have a right to do these things."

Yet those very rights in the wrong, imbalanced minds can hurt everyone else's rights as well. Your best right is the right to control your own future. Unforgiveness keeps your rights in the hands of those who abused and hurt you.

OBJECTIVES OF FORGIVENESS

What happens when we forgive? What's the object?

SELF-CHECK

- Unforgiveness will bring your physical and spiritual life to an end.
- Unforgiveness is a roadblock to a new life. It will bind you up in chronic grief.

How do you respond to these two statements?

_____

_____

_____

_____

Forgiveness is not synonymous with forgetting.

Forgiveness is not the same as forgetting. Have you ever tried to forget something? Unfortunately (and perhaps, sometimes, fortunately), we don't have a delete button in our brain. God doesn't say forget; he says forgive. Those are two separate words. Sometimes we will forget, but never because we tried to. When it happens, forgetting seems an act of grace, doesn't it? Maybe it is. Other times, it's as if we aren't supposed to forget. Maybe God wants us to learn from the painful memories, facing our pain so that we can grow in our godly character. But forgiving never requires that you forget.

But if I forgive the people who wronged me, doesn't that mean I'm letting them be as free as a bird? you may be thinking. *How can I do that?* This may be the biggest obstacle people have to forgiveness. It's also one of the biggest misunderstandings. Forgiveness is not releasing the person from personal, legal, or civic responsibilities for his or her actions. I see this sort of thinking quite a bit in professional counseling—child abuse and domestic abuse cases especially. I'll be asked: "Shouldn't we just forgive and not involve the authorities?" My answer is a very loud: "You've got it all wrong." Forgiveness does not suggest that you violate any of the laws of the land and short-circuit justice. They are there for our protection. Again, forgiveness is not for the person who's hurt you; it's for you. And that makes the next objective possible.

Forgiveness frees you.

Forgiveness is not about letting the other person go free; it's about releasing you to be free. Once you have experienced this freedom, once you've truly forgiven, you'll know how much power this one, small response can have on the rest of your life. It is literally moving you from shackles to wings.

You may be surprised at how forgiveness's freedom expresses itself for you. Maybe you'll see it as an outward expression. Maybe you will find yourself helping someone else. It can happen even after the most unforgivable crisis. As the people of Maryland find their own answers to the questions about the sniper attacks, perhaps they can take some lessons from the New Yorkers who searched for answers after September 11. They found relief in different forms of such forgiveness. One of the most touching volunteer duties was performed by Red Cross volunteers who spent the first few days after the attack walking Muslim children to school. In certain parts of New York City, where Muslims feared being terrorized, volunteers not only escorted Muslim children to school, but they also went to the market for Muslim women who were afraid to leave their homes.

Forgiveness is a lifestyle.

Forgiveness is not just an act or a one-time event. You may ask, "You mean I have to keep forgiving? Isn't once enough?"

Have you ever forgiven somebody, then later run into them? How did you feel? Did you feel all the old bitterness and anger creeping back in? Being human, you easily may have this happen to you. This is why forgiveness must be a lifestyle. Forgiveness is a continual process of letting God change the feelings that will continue to come—but come, hopefully, less often with each encounter. And that opens the way to the next objective of your forgiveness.

Forgiveness permits you to proceed in your grief recovery.

You're going to live with the consequences of other people's sin against you. Over that, you have no choice. But you can choose to either live with it in the bondage of bitterness, or you can live with it in the freedom of forgiveness. Just because you pretend you have had no loss doesn't mean it didn't happen. You will live with the consequences of that loss, however it happened, whoever was to blame. It's your choice then to either live in bitterness or to live in forgiveness.

Forgiveness's objective is to let God be God.

The objective of forgiveness, perhaps the true key to the entire idea, may surprise you. Think about it, though. As long as you are holding people accountable, you have left God no room to hold them accountable. After all, you're doing the job. Practicing the act of forgiveness means gradually knowing who God is and trusting him more. Leave accountability to God. He is much better at that than we are. Letting God be the great Scorekeeper allows you to focus your energies on what God is doing in your life.

SELF-CHECK

Respond to the following statements:
- Forgiveness lets you off the other person's hook.
- Forgiveness allows you to give up the score card.

_____

_____

Otherwise, you can waste so much time keeping score that you miss what God wants for your life.

ADVANCING YOUR FORGIVENESS

How do we move forward—advance—this concept of forgiveness now that we have a better grasp of what it will mean? We decide who to forgive. Let's make a short list and explore what each means to you.

Forgive those who have caused your pain and loss.

Who caused you the most pain in your loss? It could be a loved one. It could be a spouse, a mom, a dad, or a child who is older now. It could be an employer or employee. It could be somebody who robbed your dreams. It could be a terrorist. It could even be someone who has already died.

"If they are gone, surely they won't have any more effect on me, will they?" you may say. Remember, you are not forgiving them for their sake; you are forgiving them for your sake. Just because you are not around those people anymore doesn't mean they don't still have the power to hurt you. The effect of that hurt plays into a lot of different areas of your life. We're complex. Our lives are not compartmentalized. Everything affects everything else. Everyone affects everyone else. Across the room, across time. Who is the person that you need to forgive most in your loss?

SELF-CHECK

Turn back to the Personal Inventory Graph you created in chapter 3 where you listed all your losses and the intensity of the losses.

At that time, and for the remainder of your workbook's work, you were asked to concentrate on the loss in your life that led you here.

- Who or what is that? _____

Forgive yourself.

Maybe you need to forgive the most important person in your life—you. "I should forgive myself? I'm not mad at myself," you may say. Actually, some people are very angry with themselves. Addicts are a good example. They are addicted to something harmful. They chose to deal with their pain through an addictive behavior. Often, they are angry at themselves for not being able to control their behaviors, which, of course, creates more addictive behavior. Forgiving oneself may be the first step away from the addiction or, at least, the first step in dealing with what led them into the destructive behavior in the first place.

Maybe you believe you are guilty of contributing to your loss. Whether it's justified or unjustified, its effect can be devastating to you. Are you still feeling that guilt? Then forgive yourself. If you don't, your bitterness can turn inside and become the most dangerous, self-destructive aspect of your grieving process. It will definitely impede any other forgiveness efforts.

Think of it this way: Renew your mind. Put on a new "recording" about what God says about you: *You are forgiven, you are a new creature, and you are my child.* You've got to close that back door—the one to your own shame or guilt. Forgive yourself.

Forgive the professional people in your loss.

Are you angry at the professional people involved with your loss? You can be mad at your doctor who didn't keep your loved one from dying. You can be angry at the nurse or the paramedics, the police officer who didn't act quickly enough to prevent the loss, or the firefighter who couldn't go in until the police gave the clear sign. You can be angry at an entire group of people for what they did not do when some action might have made a difference. You can be angry toward the clergy for not saying the appropriate things or not responding the way you expected.

So you may find yourself not only having to forgive the person who caused you pain, or having to forgive yourself, but you may also be recognizing your need to forgive some people whose names you may not even know for their parts in your tragedy's story.

> If we confess our sins, he is faithful and just and will forgive us our sins and purify us from all righteousness.
>
> *1 John 1:9*

In fact, you may even have to explore *why* you are mad at a professional:

Question: Why am I apprehensive toward the hospital staff?

Answer: It was a doctor who was there when my mother died, and subconsciously I never forgave that doctor. I never thought anyone at the hospital did enough or was compassionate enough. Now I have distrust for doctors and other people in medicine.

Does that sound familiar? What might the story be for your loss? Whatever it is, are there such people you need to forgive?

Forgive God.

No list of forgiveness is complete without listing God. While recovering from a loss, we're only human if we find ourselves shaking our fist at the sky, saying, "God, I'm mad at you!"

God does not get upset when we acknowledge how we feel: "God, where are you? God, I'm upset, I'm frustrated, I'm tired, I'm weary; I need your help, and you don't seem to be there!" What breaks God's heart is when we walk away, reinforcing a belief that he was never there. It's not wrong to have a dialogue with God. But you need to remember that it's a two-way communication. As you share your feelings with God about how you feel, you have to also be willing to receive the love of a Father who is waiting at the other end, eager to talk with you.

Forgiving God is not the same as forgiving the person who caused you pain. It's closer to the way you'd forgive yourself. You're not forgiving God because God has done you wrong, but you are acknowledging your false or unrealistic expectations of God's role in alleviating any pain in your life. As you probably know deep down, that's not his role in his creation. So forgiving God is really a first step to being aware of your misperception of how God should act or intervene in your life. It is the first awareness of the growth potential of your grieving process. And the result is a more mature relationship with God.

ACTIVATING YOUR FORGIVENESS

Now that you know who to forgive, then how do you actually begin the forgiveness process? Talking about it just won't do it. Here are some steps to get the whole process jump-started—to activate the power of forgiveness in your life.

Anticipate distractions.

The minute you decide you're going to forgive somebody, the old tapes are going to start playing again.

PAUSE TO REFLECT

When you face difficult moments, wouldn't it be nice if you could recall God's comforting advice and wisdom? Try memorizing some of these helpful scriptures:

Anger: Ephesians 4:26
Depression: Isaiah 40:31
Fear: 2 Timothy 1:7
Finances: Philippians 4:19
Forgiveness: Ephesians 4:32
Loneliness: John 14:18
Sleeplessness: Psalm 4:8
Worry: 1 Peter 5:7

How could you forgive somebody who did such a thing!
You shouldn't forgive him. Don't you remember what he did to you?
How can you forgive him? Are you a doormat?

Suddenly, you're totally distracted from what God wanted you to do in the first place. There are always going to be reasons not to forgive. Anticipate people who will come and distract, but don't get stuck there.

Sometimes it takes a friend to help you through the distractions. If you'll allow me, I can be such a friend right now, or at least point you toward that friend. Often, people come into my office, sit down, and ask me to walk them through these very steps. So, think of the remainder of these tips as a long conversation with a friend. Talk back to them if you need to, but remember them.

Acknowledge the facts and how the loss made you feel.

You don't just pray, "I forgive them for everything they've ever done. Amen." Instead, you must be specific about what actually happened to you. It's like walking and saying at the beginning, "I know all the boulders, and none will stop me today." You don't know what's really there until you get to that place on the trail where they exist. So after stating the facts to God, tell him how the loss made you feel.

Allow the pain to surface.

Let those feelings that cause you so much pain rise to the surface. Revisit your chapter on pain, if you must. Do you feel rejected? Unworthy? Deserted? Dirty? There is some real emotion there, and that is what God wants to heal—the hurt that you're covering up. I call it the "slime factor" of life. If you don't deal with the slime, it never quite gets cleaned up. It just keeps getting smeared all over everything.

Adopt an attitude of forgiveness as a decision of obedience.

Forgiveness is not a feeling; it's a hard-won act of obedience. No one—not you, not me, not anyone—will ever feel like forgiving somebody who has hurt us. You may say, "I'll forgive them when I feel like forgiving." But you will never get there. You will be stepping around forgiveness for the rest of your life. You'll never want to let go of the debt owed you. But that may be what you have to give up to have the peace that you so desperately want. It starts with a decision to forgive—not a feeling, but a decision.

Forgiveness is taking the legitimate debt the person or event has caused and depositing it into God's hands. You know you have forgiven when you can honestly say where the debt is. If it is between you and the person, it's time to revisit the steps to forgiveness; there is still a boulder of bitterness there. If the debt owed is with God, you know you have removed the boulders and the path is clear.

Repeat after me: *I choose to leave it with God and go on into a new life.*

If that is what it takes to live again, isn't that worth doing? Sometimes you just have to remind yourself of the benefits of sacrificing your hurt for your future. Choose to live with the circumstances of the event without seeking revenge or vengeance, wrath or restitution. You're not looking for justice. Leave that to the authorities and to the Highest Authority. You're looking for obedience and for that relationship with your Creator that inspired David to write Psalm 23. And when you can do that, you will be greater for it. That's when you are in the presence of God and are ready to move forward in your healing.

We've now pushed the start button on the forgiveness process—deeply exploring the absolutes, the effects, the objectives, the advancement, and the activation of this all-important part of the road to recovery. Now you will have to keep pushing it for a while to keep it going, but if you do, you'll be on your way, each step closer to the healthy, positive end of your grieving journey. You'll be on your way home.

Work It Out

Sometimes you need a friend to help you get your forgiveness process started and steadily moving on. Think of yourself in my office, listening to me ask you these questions and waiting for your responses. Say a quick prayer for yourself and then read the following:

1. Who are the ones who've caused you pain—who are you mad at? Include everyone you've felt has added to your pain. List their names or their occupations and what part they played. What specifically did each person do to you?

_____

_____

2. Now, stop and pray for each person you listed. Next, pray for yourself. How did that make you feel?

_____

_____

3. List all the emotions that the tragedy has created in your life. Seeing them written can help you manage them.

_____

_____

_____

_____

4. Can you give to God the debt owed by those people for your loss? *But I've already forgiven them,* you may have thought. Maybe you have, but ask yourself, *Where is the debt?* Forgiveness is a process. It's an act of obedience instead of a feeling. Where is the debt today for you?

_____

_____

5. Reread Psalm 23. What do you think David had to give up to feel the presence of God so deeply when he wrote this wonderful song?

_____

_____

6. How does David's experience relate to what you've learned about your own feelings at this moment?

_____

_____

Grief Recovery Journal

Date _____

Dear _____ :

This is how I feel right now:

_____

_____

_____

_____

_____

_____

_____

_____

_____

_____

This is what I've discovered today:

_____

_____

_____

_____

_____

_____

_____

_____

_____

_____

This is what I still question today:

_____

_____

_____

_____

_____

_____

_____

_____

_____

_____

_____

Extra space to finish your thoughts, if needed:

_____

_____

_____

_____

_____

_____

_____

_____

_____

_____

For additional encouragement, listen to
Number 12 on the *Grief Recovery Workbook CD*

Chapter 12

Coming Home

Raymond Lanigan was abandoned by his mother when he was six months old. He was the last of nine children born in ten years. In 1960, the year Raymond was born, his father began serving a sentence in the New Jersey State Prison. So this young mother was left to raise nine children, five boys and four girls, entirely alone. One day, when he was ten months old, Raymond's mother went out for bread and never came home.

His mother had told Raymond's ten-year-old sister to watch all the children while she went to the market. As the days went by, the girl fed the kids with whatever food was left in the house, until it was all gone. Finally, at the end of a week, she went next door to ask the neighbors if they had seen her mother, still believing she would return. The neighbors immediately alerted the police, who were already familiar with the dire family situation. Raymond's father, a long-haul truck driver, was serving a one-year prison term for failure to support his family, after years of neglect due to his drinking. So the children had been abandoned, in reality, by both parents.

That day the nine children were all separated, Raymond's brothers and sisters were put into foster homes while his youngest sister and he were hospitalized due to malnutrition, dehydration, and infected sores from the neglect.

His father would die four years later of cirrhosis of the liver. His mother was never found.

Raymond was not even aware he had brothers and sisters until he was nearly twenty-six. Catholic Charities had taken him directly from the hospital as a baby and placed him in foster care with a family who ultimately adopted him. As it turned out, that included an extremely different life from that experienced by Raymond's birth siblings. He grew up loved and a part of a normal American family. And when he grew up, he went to college and got married.

Then one day in 1986, as he and his wife planned for the arrival of their first child, she asked him what he knew of his family. Her doctor was asking questions about their medical histories. But Raymond knew nothing more than his birth surname and his birthplace.

Finally, he agreed to make an attempt to find out more for the sake of his first child. And that one small attempt set into motion a chain of events that led him back into his past.

Since he knew his birth surname, he went to a nearby university library and researched microfiche of old New Jersey phone books. In the 1960 Trenton phone book, he found three Lanigans listed. He picked up the phone and dialed. He called the first number; it was disconnected. He called the second one; no response. When he dialed the third phone number, a man answered.

"Yes, our name is Lanigan," he said.

"Can you tell me the history of the Lanigans in Trenton?" he asked the man. "Do you remember a time when someone might have been killed or died in the family, and maybe a child was born during it all? I'm a Lanigan, and I'm trying to find out if I'm part of your family."

The man was abrupt. "I don't know. My father might. This is his house. He's been in this town for years, but he's in Florida right now vacationing. If he knows anything, I'll give him your number and he'll call you."

With that, Raymond let it go. He told his wife that the phone call was all he could do. A few weeks later, he received a call. A woman on the other end of the line began to ask him question after question. Was his name Raymond Lanigan? Was he born in New Jersey? Had he lived in Trenton? Was he born in 1960?

Finally he stopped her and asked, "What's this about? Why are you calling?"

The voice went silent. After a few seconds, he could hear the woman begin to cry.

"We've looked for you for twenty-five years, and we have finally found you," she said. The woman was his sister. She began to tell him the entire story. Raymond Lanigan could hardly believe his ears. "How many have you found?" he asked when he finally found his voice.

"You're the sixth, and there are still three left," she said. Two of the younger brothers were still "missing," as was his youngest sister. "But now that we've found you, we want to have a reunion," she said. "Can you come to New Jersey?"

He could and did. During Easter week of 1986, he met the brothers and sisters who had kept in touch. And now, he wanted to know everything—and find his lost siblings. The family was able to show him his father's grave, and they believed they knew where their mother's sister might live, although they had never found the courage to approach her. But they now decided to go. So that week, after waiting nearly twenty-six years, they began a journey to find all their brothers and sisters.

They knocked on their aunt's door and waited in silent anticipation. The door opened and they met their mother's sister. She invited them in and told them what she recalled of that day long ago. Then she paused and told them one thing more. Years before, she was certain she had seen their mother in the Irish area of Upper Manhattan, living on the streets. But when she had approached the homeless woman, the woman had answered, "I don't have a family, I don't have any children, and I don't know you." But the aunt was certain that the homeless person was their mother, her lost sister. And anything seemed possible that week. So the next day, despite the intervening years and the odds against that homeless woman being his mother, Raymond and his siblings actually traveled to that specific Manhattan area on the off chance that they might see their mother. They didn't, but instead of being discouraged, they went back to one of the sister's homes, turned on the television, and watched the next installment of their family reunion miracle unfold.

By that time, they had already been the subjects of numerous features in newspapers as well as local television news, both in California and New Jersey. Local media in Raymond's hometown had heard about his trip, and within a matter of days, the saga became a national human-interest story on NBC News—and it aired during the week of his visit to Trenton.

The timing of this new media exposure would produce two little miracles of human kindness for Raymond Lanigan's amazing reunion journey.

The first came within a few hours of the program's airing. The phone rang at his sister's home where he was staying. The woman on the other end introduced herself: "I'm the social worker who handled the case twenty-five years ago," she said. "I handled the adoption of your brother who you just found, and the adoption of your sister. Have you located her yet?"

No, his sister told the woman.

The social worker explained that she had worked hard to keep the babies together, trying to find someone who would take two infants. She hadn't been successful, though, and it had always bothered her. Now, all these years later, she was extremely glad for another chance to help. "I can't give you the information," the social worker added, "but this is what we can do. I know her number, so I'll call her. If she's interested in getting hold of you, she can."

Very soon, the phone rang again, and on the other end of the line was the missing baby sister. She had lived in Trenton her whole life, adopted by a family only a few miles away.

So, incredibly, within a matter of hours, Raymond's youngest sister appeared at his sister's door. Raymond had only two more brothers left to find. Figuring that they had, like the other Lanigans, stayed in New Jersey, the Lanigan siblings went, en masse, to the nearest Department of Motor Vehicles office, hoping against hope that the officials might give them the information.

The woman they approached at the DMV counter was abrupt. "Go down to the end of the counter and wait for me." So they paraded over there and waited. Finally, the woman appeared again, and this time she was anything but abrupt. "I saw you on television. I could lose my job for this, but the story has so moved me, it would be worth it. Here's the address of your brother."

They all drove to the address they were given. The woman who opened the door was their brother's wife. She picked up her phone and called her husband at work. He immediately came home to a house full of new family. And he soon told his new siblings where the last brother could be found as well. As the two grew up in orphanages, foster care, and reform schools, they, at least, had been able to keep up with each other. So, on Sunday, the day before Raymond was to fly home, eight of the nine long-lost Lanigans had one last reunion get-together at a restaurant. And in walked the last brother to make the reunion complete. After a quarter-century, the Lanigan siblings were reunited on Easter Sunday, 1986.

For a very long time, Raymond was overwhelmed by the new facts of his life. He was a Christian and a church member, and he truly believed and had accepted the gift of a personal God through Christ. It was all valid and true and had been for years. But that reunion miracle was the first time he recognized the grace of God in action. In his family's story of tragedy and restoration, he experienced the first act of dramatic redemption he had ever known. Not until that moment had he understood the depth of God's love. Suddenly, being a Christian took on a brand-new meaning. That God could take something that was so broken and put it all back together so dramatically and so quickly was proof-positive of divine love and all its powerful possibilities.

He went back to school, this time for a theological degree, and soon began to see that he had a heart for helping people in crisis. And that work would propel him all the way to Ground Zero. During those months working in Manhattan, he thought about his mother many times. One night while walking through the Ground Zero area, he saw some blankets and a grocery cart full of the kinds of things collected by a person living on the streets. "They must have belonged to a homeless person killed in the building's collapse," he commented to a fellow worker who knew his story. "For all I know, that could have been my mother."

Odds are it wasn't, of course; forty years is an impossibly long time to live on the streets of New York City. But what would he say to his mother if they were reunited? "It's okay, Mom. God took care of me."

I want to tell you a second story about Ray Lanigan.

Days after the World Trade Center attack, I found myself at Ground Zero working as a crisis chaplain digging with the firefighters. One night, I had just finished a twelve-hour shift at Ground Zero. It was 2:00 A.M. in New York City. Pastor Ryan, a fellow We Care team member, and I were staying at a respite center on Staten Island, so we decided to take the ferry back.

On our way, we saw an elderly woman walking stiffly, slowly, down the dark, deserted streets. And beside her shuffled a small, dark-haired boy with an innocent, couch-potato look to him, perhaps ten or eleven years old, head down, sniffling back tears. They were both carrying full, black garbage bags.

Everything about the scene looked odd. An old woman and a young boy, in the middle of the night, walking down the streets of Lower Manhattan, carrying plastic bags.

"Can we help you with your bags, ma'am?" we asked after introducing ourselves.

"Oh, thank you so much," she said.

"Where are you going?" we asked.

"Staten Island. We took the subway all the way from Brooklyn."

"If you don't mind our asking, why are you out at this time of the night? It's cold, wet, and obviously not safe."

"Oh, you just won't believe it," she answered, sighing. "My daughter is a drug addict, and tonight she kicked him out of the house."

"Him?" I asked, pointing to the boy.

"Him." The boy hung his head even lower.

"She said he couldn't live with her anymore," the grandmother went on. "She called me and told me to come get him, because she was going to put him out on the street."

My heart went out to the boy. He was probably carrying everything he owned in the world in those black garbage bags. This night was never going to leave him. His own mother was literally throwing him away.

So while my fellow chaplain encouraged the grandmother, I introduced myself to the boy. I put my arm around him and let him talk. His mother was having trouble with drugs, he said, and had just moved him from New Jersey, but now she didn't want him anymore. And he didn't know where his father was. But it was going to be better now because he was finally going to his grandmother's.

I wanted to offer him some tiny bit of hope and comfort. So I started telling him the story about a little boy who was born Raymond Lanigan years ago, whose mother didn't want him either, and who had abandoned him. I told him how the boy almost died, and would have, except for a sister about this boy's age. I told him how he had lived in New Jersey, too, and how he would move a long way away without knowing what truly happened. When I finished the story, I said, "You want to know what happened to that little boy when he grew up?"

The boy perked up. "Yeah, what happened?"

"That little boy is here in New York City. He has been at Ground Zero helping people."

The little boy smiled for the first time. "Really?" he said, "*really?* He's here?"

"Yes, he's right here," I said. "I'm that little boy."

The boy's eyes grew wide, and then he began to cry. I hugged him with all of my might. I told him that there would be many nights he would lay his head on his pillow and cry. He'd wonder how his mom could do this to him. He'd wonder what was wrong with him, what he had done to make her quit loving him. I told him I knew because I had done that, too. And yet God had sent somebody just like him over three thousand miles to bump into him in the middle of this one night of all nights. And if God cared enough to do that, then in the days to come, God would surely continue to send people to help him, if he would just keep looking.

We talked with the grandmother and the boy for a little longer, doing all we could to comfort them before we prayed for them and parted at the ferry.

As we moved to take our seats, my mind churning with both his story and mine, I prayed a small, silent prayer: *Thanks for letting me, of all people, happen to be right here for this one little boy.* And then a thought hit me so hard I stopped in my tracks:

Did I meet that boy for him—or for *me?* Or for *both* of us?

I moved to the railing and gazed across the river toward my birthplace. I had shared my story many times, but never so close to "home"—in all the meanings that word implies. *Ray,* I thought, *you've come full-circle home. Look where you've been led.* Here I was, in the middle of the night, within sight of Ground Zero, happening to meet a boy—a mirror image of myself—who had nothing to do with the World Trade Center disaster . . . and yet everything to do with it. It was as if God were saying, *Look at what I can do. I want to redeem* every *part of this.*

So many people came to New York City after September 11, led there for many reasons, most of us following some inner compass. Whether I, Ray Giunta, was there would probably not have made a monumental difference in the big picture; others would certainly have done the same meaningful work I had had the chance to do. But whether I, Ray Lanigan Giunta, was there at 2:00 A.M., blocks from the site of that enormous disaster, to walk into the life of a small boy's disaster, did seem to make an incredible, stunning difference.

That, suddenly, seemed the deepest reason for why I had come to New York: I came for that little boy—and I also came for the man who once was that little boy. I had finally come all the way home.

You need to know there is an end to the journey, that your grief recovery is a God-given process that includes every last area we've discussed in the pages of this workbook. You have to understand your loss and face your fear, your loneliness, your guilt, your pain, and your anger. But to finally come all the way home, you have to open yourself to God's part in both the pain and the power.

Your goal when you found yourself in your own personal grief wilderness and took your first steps down the road to recovery was to complete the journey. To complete it by embracing once again the abundant life God promised, the growth your pain has allowed, and the rich rewards that maturity offers for your future, whatever your past grief has been. Your grief process can be that powerful, if you've allowed the process to lead you all the way here—all the way home.

> "I have come that they may have life, and have it to the full."
>
> *John 10:10*

But the journey doesn't really end there, either. Completing the grief cycle doesn't mean that you will never take this journey again. It's a constant journey but one that has a definite end. Sounds like a paradox, but it isn't.

So how do you know you are home?

I've heard the wonder expressed in many ways, but the main thought is the same:

I'd just like to get back to life.
Can't I just return to some semblance of life, some sense of what I had before?
If I could just have control over this life again. . . .
If I could just have one good day, I'd be so happy.

Coming home is when you come to that place where you say: "I want to live again."

Remember the signposts to recovery in chapter 2? It's time now to study them closely. I explained them in detail early in your grief recovery work to give you a glimpse of what lies at the end of your journey. Now that you are so much closer to that destination, it's time to reevaluate where you are in the process. Turn back to pages 27–32 for a full explanation of any of the signposts. Let's review those signposts to recovery to see how close you are to "coming home":

NINE SIGNPOSTS TO RECOVERY

1. Recovery is feeling better.
2. Recovery is reclaiming your circumstances instead of your circumstances claiming you.
3. Recovery is finding new meaning for living without the fear of future abandonment.
4. Recovery is being able to enjoy fond memories without having them stir up painful feelings of loss, guilt, and remorse.
5. Recovery is acknowledging that it is all right to feel bad from time to time and to be able to talk about those feelings.
6. Recovery is being able to forgive others when they say or do things that are painful.
7. Recovery is realizing that your ability to talk about the loss or your experience helps others coping with their loss.
8. Recovery is a return to the desire to live again and provide for the people in your life.
9. Recovery is a renewal of faith in God and a rebirth of hope in your life.

Do any of those sound more familiar now? More possible? If so, it is at this crucial step that your thoughts and activities move beyond the event. That's what "coming home" means in the context of your grief journey. There will be a moment when you know you have come home.

COMING HOME MEANS . . .

Let's explore what coming home looks like. How will you know when you've arrived?

Unwrapping the Grave Clothes

Whatever your loss, it was a death of some sort. It was either an end of some loved one's life, or the end of a relationship or a precious trust. But you've been experiencing a death. There is a point when we need to unwrap the grave clothes.

Remember the biblical story of Lazarus? You may know the story, but did you notice

SELF-CHECK

How far along are you on the recovery road?

- List those signposts that you are most dramatically seeing in your life at this moment:

_____

_____

_____

_____

this important part of it? Lazarus was dead in the tomb for four days. Jesus waited before he went to Lazarus's grave, and many have preached that Jesus waited so witnesses would have a total dependence on him and would really know that Lazarus was dead.

But that is not the part of the story that I want to focus on. It's enough to say that Lazarus was dead. Not only was he dead, he had been dead so long in that hot climate, his loved ones were upset when Jesus told them to roll back the stone. They were actually afraid the body would stink.

But when Christ called out: "Lazarus, come out!" Lazarus obeyed. He came back to life and he walked out of his grave. I can only picture what it must have been like to see this man bound hand to foot, wrapped all the way up and around his face, not even an opening for his eyes. So Lazarus was alive. He was resurrected by Jesus Christ, but he had a little problem. He was still all bound up, unable to help himself, even after being brought back to life. Jesus said a very interesting thing at this point. He had just brought his friend back from the dead; obviously, he could have also taken care of the cloth that bound him. But instead, after Lazarus came forth out of the tomb, Christ said to those who were standing there: "Take off the grave clothes and let him go."

It had to take a lot of guts, and a lot of love, for them to walk near their strange, no-longer-dead friend, hobbling from the grave where they had buried him, and start taking off those wrappings. But if those people hadn't been obedient, Lazarus would have died again, suffocating to death.

Can you see the lesson in this story? There comes a point in all of our pain when it's time to take off the grave clothes or we will smother in them. God wants you to know that once he resurrects you, the grave clothes have to come off. We have to stop living in that life with the old stinky cloth on us. Coming home means removing the grave clothes so we can move on.

Living Recovered

Are you at the point of wanting your life to begin again? Can you see that soon you may be at that place, even if you aren't right now? If so, you're almost ready to begin living recovered. Because that's what coming home really is. Coming home is living recovered. Living recovered means reclaiming or regaining control of your life.

Coming home is walking in the abundant life promised by God. Living recovered is realizing that moments are yours again, that you are able to enjoy memories that formerly only reminded you of the loss's pain. You keep those memories but slowly say good-bye to the pain.

> "Take off the grave clothes and let him go."
>
> *John 11:44*

Developing New Living Patterns

Coming home is developing new living patterns and deciding what to do with the extra time. That's probably the hardest part about loss, especially if you are a widow. You had all this time you spent with your spouse: You ate together, worked together, slept together, walked together, and played together. The two of you did all those things together, and now you're alone. But you still have all that time. Time is the one thing that never disappears, does it? You have to decide. Coming home is deciding what you are going to do with all that time. It's a real thing; it's not going to change. You may have had a loss, but you still have twenty-four hours in the day.

Many great support and recovery groups, many great missions and ministries, have been developed by people who have experienced loss and have now channeled that time into these worthy causes. They've used the extra time, along with new wisdom, in a positive way.

Cultivating New Friendships

Coming home is cultivating new friendships. You will now begin to form friendships without that person you've lost. This is also true if you are divorced or separated. It's such a hard thing to trust again, to reach out and say you're going to risk your heart again. But God didn't put us on the earth just to sit in our house and be alone.

You may be thinking, *I like this loneliness.*

My response? You don't like your loneliness; you've accepted your grief as a badge. And it's time to come home and open yourself up to new relationships.

Developing New Traditions

Coming home is developing new traditions because they help us to accept the reality of a loss. A man committed suicide and left his wife and children alone. Months later, the wife came to me about a decision she had to make. "It's almost Thanksgiving time," she said, "and I don't know what I'm going to do with the kids. We were a traditional family. Thanksgiving was formal and wonderful in our house. But I can't bear to set the table this year. His spot will be empty."

"Well, what would you like to do?" I asked.

She said, "I don't even know if this is right or not, but I'm thinking of just flying the kids to Disneyland and spending Thanksgiving there. Do you think that would be okay?"

I responded: "I think that would be a marvelous idea. I think you could make that a new tradition in your home." And that's just what they did—they spent every Thanksgiving for years at Disneyland. Coming home is no longer suppressing or denying the loss. Coming home is accepting the reality and re-making traditions to work for your future instead of the past.

Reaching Out to Others

Part of coming home is reaching out to others. You'll want to be the one who is unwrapping others' grave clothes. And that's the way it was meant to be. Christ wants us to begin to unwrap the grave clothes still binding others—as soon as we are able. When you begin to share what you learned in your own grief process and what has helped you, then you'll know you're on your way home for sure.

Never fear, there will be many opportunities to help others. They have always been there: others who are suppressing their anger, feeling their guilt, isolating themselves and feeling alone and helpless—just as you did. When you see them, you know you're ready to come all the way home. And you'll know now what to do and what to say.

AVOIDING THE PITFALLS

You must understand, however, even though you're coming home, even though you're in this final stage of your grief recovery, there will be more than a few setbacks waiting for you. Awareness is your best defense. Avoid the pitfalls ahead with the following tips:

Take Your Time

Don't rush yourself, because grief is unique. A person once said to me, "I read that it takes two years to get over grief. So after two years, I should be better."

"Well, if it happens for you in two years," I said, "that's fine. But if it doesn't, that's fine too." Grief is unique. You may feel better in two weeks, and that's okay. You may feel better in ten years, and that's okay. As long as you're walking with God on the journey, as long as you are processing as you go, it's fine. So take your time. Don't let people rush your grief. It's your grief. It's unique to you.

Try to Avoid Self-Pity

When I complete my daily walk, I leave the forest's dusty path and begin the final leg to my home up the winding hill. Sometimes I'm tired and want to hitch a ride or just stop and rest. It is then I think, *Why did I walk today?* You'll likewise be tempted now and then to invite yourself to your very own pity party. You're not alone; it happens so much that I'd be surprised if it didn't happen to you.

But we all need to be aware of self-pity when it comes. It's not the work of the Lord. It will distract you from processing your grief. Use your new knowledge about your grief process whenever you feel you're in danger of leaving home to go to that pity party. Because, if you avoid that party, you have a better celebration awaiting: As I reach the knoll on my walk and see my destination ahead, I'm reminded that I'm home, and the sense of accomplishment is amazing. I've completed another journey! You can experience the same peace if you'll stick with the journey.

The biggest self-pity danger can be those special dates on your calendar—the anniversary date of your loss, the date of the divorce or the separation, the date of your wedding or child's birthday...and on and on. Don't be discouraged. Feeling vulnerable on those days of the year is part of the process. Feeling less vulnerable as the days go by is part of coming home and a normal part of the end of the journey.

Another danger is the same one that's been a problem throughout your journey—other people's remarks. Even though you've journeyed through this process of grief, people will still say some hateful, hurtful things. Because people are ignorant about grief, they will say ignorant things—and perhaps the same old things that have hurt you all along your journey. Don't let those remarks plunge you back into self-pity. You are doing so well. Keep on coming home.

Be open, however, to the encouragement all around you—the good things people can say to you—especially when you have taken a self-destructive step back. Such encouragement is meant for your benefit. It's easy at that point to be angry at such reminders. So you want to recognize the difference whenever you can.

Work It Out

Think about other pitfalls you can see in this last stretch of the journey. You have learned enough through the course of this workbook to identify your own sensitive situations. Now is the time to keep your eyes wide open for them.

Keep this book open to this page, and as you go through the next few days and weeks, write down the things you notice that could cause a setback. Being aware of those pot-holes in your recovery road will keep you safe:

1. _____
2. _____
3. _____
4. _____
5. _____

CONTINUING THE JOURNEY

You will continue the journey of the grieving process even after arriving "home." It's a good journey, though, once you're at this place. You'll know all the signposts and all the pitfalls, and you'll be better for having been brave enough to learn the way. Remember these points and embrace them on your daily walk into your future:

1. Understand your continuing need.
2. Reuse tools learned for the journey.
3. Be honest with yourself about your fears.
4. Have a plan and keep using it as long as needed.

> "He will wipe every tear from their eyes. There will be no more death or mourning or crying or pain, for the old order of things has passed away."
>
> *Revelation 21:4*

LIFE WILL NEVER BE THE SAME

One last word of caution and encouragement: Recovery doesn't have to be perfect. You won't hear, "You're fixed now. Good-bye!" But there is one thing about your future you should understand: You will never be the same.

People will say this often and in varied ways. But they say it in a negative way, usu-ally. Grief recovery, though, means you can say it in a positive sense: "Life is never going to be the same." The relationship is over, the job has ended, the child has died, your husband has gone to be with the Lord. So those people are right: Life is not going to be the same. But neither is your relationship with God. And the plan has always been so.

Each day is like that, in small ways as well as big ones. Isn't it? But dramatically, so is the grief recovery process. The grief process is designed into our nature as a great leap forward—if we allow the plan to unfold. And that is what you have done within the safe confines of this workbook.

Through the loss that you have experienced and your healthy recovery efforts, your relationship with God will be different. You will be in a different place spiritually because of the things that have happened in your life. And that can be good. Yes, it *is* good. You will know God better, and you are learning to listen to his voice in a new way. Yes, you will be a different person—a better person. That's a powerful message, a message that transforms lives. When you know it has transformed your life, then you know you have come all the way home.

Grief Recovery Journal

Date _____

Dear _____ :

This is how I feel right now:

_____

_____

_____

_____

_____

_____

_____

_____

_____

_____

This is what I've discovered today:

_____

_____

_____

_____

_____

_____

_____

_____

_____

_____

This is what I still question today:

_____

_____

_____

_____

_____

_____

_____

_____

_____

_____

_____

Extra space to finish your thoughts, if needed:

_____

_____

_____

_____

_____

_____

_____

_____

_____

_____

_____

For additional encouragement, listen to Number 13 on the *Grief Recovery Workbook CD*

Appendix 1

Children's Grief

I met Tyler early one morning as he sat in his grandmother's lap at a neighbor's home. Tyler had been asleep in an upstairs bedroom with his mother, Jamie, who had moved back home with her family to escape a violent relationship. Having done the proper things—moving away, obtaining a restraining order, staying away from the violent father and boyfriend—she must have felt safe that day. As Jamie's father left for work that morning for his daily commute to his job in a nearby city, he could never have imagined what he would come home to. Shortly after he left, the estranged boyfriend took a large brick and smashed the back patio glass door to the residence. Before Tyler's grandmother could get to the landing, the man was up the stairs and headed for the room where Tyler and his mother were sleeping. In a moment, Jamie was dead, sent to eternity by one who claimed he loved her. As he turned the gun on Tyler, the boy's grandmother rushed in and saved his life by grabbing the gun. But the boyfriend somehow fired the gun several times into his own body, fulfilling his original plan of a murder-suicide. Tyler had seen it all.

In the years since that day, my family has come to love Tyler and we've all been involved in his life. He has become a brother and son to our family. I see Tyler often because he attends the local Christian school. He has come a long way since the event that claimed both his mother and father, and by God's grace, he will be a boy who grows up to know a God who is always faithful.

I think of Tyler when I consider the unique needs of children who must handle traumatic loss. They grieve in different ways than adults. Adults recognize they're grieving, whereas children might have no understanding of what they are feeling. Children need special attention after a significant loss. Even very young children who cannot comprehend the meaning of death still may sense that something is wrong. These little ones are more complex and honest about their feelings than adults; however, their reactions are harder to predict. Children's reactions to trauma will involve not only the impact of the event on their lives, but a sense of crisis over their parents' and teachers' reactions.

A central theme that emerges in children's responses to disastrous events is that they experience the fear of death and destruction. Particularly influential in the young child's grief experience are the terror and reality of overwhelming physical forces that seem to have rendered the all-powerful, adult parents frightened and powerless.

Adults feel immediate intensity of loss for a long period of time. Children experience brief reaction periods several times a day, grieving in a cyclical pattern. Adults may take two to five years to resolve a grief. Children reevaluate at each stage of their development.

GRIEF RESPONSES IN CHILDREN

Each child will react uniquely and may exhibit some of these behaviors or reactions appropriate to their age. Use this as a guide to help yourself identify children's grief:

Infants and Toddlers (Birth to 2 years old)

1. Exhibits high levels of anxiety as seen in agitated/restless behavior, excessive crying, thumb-sucking, biting, and throwing objects.
2. Unlikely to retain a strong mental memory of trauma, but may retain a physical memory.

Preschoolers (3 to 5 years old)

1. May not have the same level of denial as adults, so will react to the catastrophe more swiftly.

2. Releases internal conflicts through dramatic play about the traumatic event—sometimes to the distress of parents or adults.

3. Exhibits behaviors of "separation anxiety" toward caretakers, including physically holding on to adults, not wanting to sleep alone, wanting to be held, and excessive crying in absence of the primary caretaker/parent.

4. Becomes mute, withdrawn, and still.

5. Has extended periods of sadness.

6. Shows noticeable regression in physical independence, such as refusal to dress, feed, or wash self; may forget toilet training; may wet the bed.

7. Suffers from sleep disturbances, particularly nightmares.

8. Sees changes in daily routine as a threat.

9. Is unable to understand death and its permanency.

10. Has feelings of anger and rejection.

School-age Children (6 to 10 years old)

1. Continues to use dramatic play/reenactment as the primary method of expression; other forms seen in art, drawing, dance, or music.

2. Has difficulty concentrating in school.

3. Exhibits radical changes in behavior (for instance, the normally quiet child suddenly becomes active and noisy; the normally active child becomes lethargic).

4. Has fantasies about the traumatic event with a "rescue" ending.

5. Withdraws trust from adults.

6. Shows delay in growth toward independence.

7. Complains of such things as headaches, stomachaches, and dizziness.

8. Has increasing difficulty in controlling own behavior.

9. Regresses to previous developmental stage.

Preadolescence (Girls: 12-14 years old; Boys: 10-12 years old)

1. Becomes more childlike in attitude.

2. Harbors anger at unfairness of the disaster.

3. Feels euphoria and excitement at survival.

4. Attributes symbolic meaning to predisaster events and assigns symbolic reasons to postdisaster survival.

5. Suppresses thoughts and feelings to avoid confronting disaster.

6. Becomes judgmental about own and others' behavior.

7. Develops a sense of impending doom for the future.

8. Feels a sense of meaninglessness of existence.

9. Manifests psychosomatic illnesses/symptoms.

Adolescents (12 to 18 years old)

1. Resembles adult post-traumatic stress disorder reactions.

2. Feelings of anger, shame, betrayal.

3. Acts out frustration through rebellious conduct in school.

4. Transitions rapidly into the adult world to flee a sense of disaster and establish control over environment.

5. Becomes judgmental of own and others' behavior.

6. Contributes survival to a sense of immortality.

7. Is suspicious and guarded in reaction to others.

8. Develops eating and sleeping disorders.

9. Is plagued with depression.

10. Loses control of impulses, becoming a threat to others.

11. Suffers alcohol and drug abuse as a result of perceived meaningless.

12. Fears that the disaster or tragedy will repeat, adding to sense of impending doom.

13. Develops psychosomatic illnesses/symptoms.

COPING STRATEGIES TO HELP CHILDREN

Answer their questions as honestly and simply as you can.

1. Allow them to express their true feelings to you. Don't assume everyone is processing the loss in the same way.

2. Talk to the children about the tragedy, addressing the irrationality of tragedy.

3. Encourage reenactments and dramatic play about the event—painting, drawing, writing.

Reaffirm the child's security and your dedication to their safety.

1. Love and care for them; that's their primary need.
2. Allow extra time for those having a difficult time dealing with their loss.
3. Reaffirm the future and talk in hopeful terms about future events to help build trust and faith in their world again.

Be patient.

1. Prepare for regressive behaviors and accept the manifestation of aggression and anger as normal, especially in the early phases after tragedy.
2. Let them talk on their own terms and levels. However, it may be helpful to ask them to consider what other children are feeling or thinking about the event, if applicable.
3. Tell them that you care about what they are feeling.

Learn to read between the lines.

1. Listen for cues that might tell you what is bothering them (feelings of guilt, anger, depression, and so forth).
2. Get professional assistance as warranted.
3. Encourage them to ask questions to help process their emotions.

Appendix 2

For Those Who Want to Learn Compassionate Crisis Care

Much of what you've learned in the pages of the workbook, you can apply to helping others as well as yourself. However, here are a few extra things to remember when practicing compassionate crisis care:

1. Practice Dedicated Listening

   Lora Watson once wrote,

   "Listening is seeing invisible tears that are never cried.
   Listening is knowing impossible dreams that are never tried.
   Listening is hearing weary sighs that are never sighed.
   Listening is Love."

   Remain quiet. Remember, God gave you two ears and only one mouth so you could listen twice as much as you speak.

   Never suggest that the relationship can be replaced.

   Never be horrified if the individual mentions how the person died.

   Never try to change the subject.

   Never say that you know how he or she feels. Although you may be tempted to say this because you have had a similar loss, remember that grief is unique to each individual because it is based on their relationship with who or what is gone.

2. Practice Compassionate Talking

Talk only after a great deal of listening.

If you've listened well, you'll know what to say.

Don't be afraid to speak.

Don't over-spiritualize the conversation.

Avoid asking awkward questions: "How are you feeling?"

Allow the person to continue speaking anytime.

Listen again. He or she will share their feelings, and that will aid your responses.

3. Don't Ask—DO

See a need and fill it.

Remember practical needs, as outlined in chapter 3.

4. Make Contact

Use touch. A tremendous amount of healing can come through a touch—of hand, a hug, a hand on a shoulder.

Touch only as a normal progression of listening, talking, and doing.

Gestures often convey a message as effectively as a word.

Eye contact and body language are extremely important.

Be careful not to overdo—or touch inappropriately.

5. More Helpful Hints

Take your clues from the person who is grieving.

Let the grieving person set the agenda of the conversation.

Talk of the deceased when they do. Don't avoid saying their loved one's name.

Always keep in mind that grieving people are very forgiving—when you make a mistake, apologize and move forward.

Whenever you promise to do something, do it.

When you find you don't have something to say, try: "I'm here for you and I want to help."

Take your time and relax. Remember, God is doing his work through you.

Grief Recovery Library

Here is a short list of books you might find helpful on your journey. For specific topics or types of loss, inquire at your local bookstore or contact one of the organizations mentioned in Appendix 4.

General Grief/Loss

Good Grief: A Constructive Approach to the Problem of Loss by Granger E. Westberg (Fortress Press)

Healing Your Grieving Heart by Alan D. Wolfelt (Companion Press)

The Problem of Pain by C. S. Lewis (HarperSanFrancisco)

Recovering from the Losses of Life by H. Norman Wright (Fleming H. Revell)

A Path Through Suffering: Discovering the Relationship Between God's Mercy and Our Pain by Elisabeth Elliot (Vine Books)

Emotions: Can You Trust Them? by James Dobson (Regal Books)

When God Doesn't Make Sense by James Dobson (Tyndale House)

Where Is God When It Hurts? by Philip Yancey (Zondervan)

Disappointment with God by Philip Yancey (Zondervan)

Trusting God Through Tears: A Story to Encourage by Jehu Thomas Burton & Dan B. Allender (Baker)

Holding On to Hope: A Pathway Through Suffering to the Heart of God by Nancy Guthrie (Tyndale House)

Children's Grief

Helping Children Cope with Grief by Alan D. Wolfelt (Accelerated Development)

Helping Children Grieve by Theresa M. Huntley (Augsburg Fortress)

Death

Facing the Death of Someone You Love by Elisabeth Elliot (Good News Publishers)

A Grief Observed by C. S. Lewis (HarperSanFrancisco)

On Death and Dying by Elisabeth Kubler-Ross (Scribner)

Anger/Forgiveness

When You Can't Say "I Forgive You": Breaking the Bonds of Anger and Hurt by Grace Ketterman (NavPress)

Anger Is a Choice by Tim LaHaye & Bob Phillips (Zondervan)

Healing for a Bitter Heart: Releasing the Power of Forgiveness by Charles R. Gerber & Gary Collins (College Press Publishing Company)

The Other Side of Love: Handling Anger in a Godly Way by Gary Chapman (Moody Press)

The Healing Path: How the Hurts in Your Past Can Lead You to a More Abundant Life by Dan B. Allender (Waterbrook Press)

Depression/Loneliness

How to Win Over Depression by Tim LaHaye (Zondervan)

The Path of Loneliness: Finding Your Way Through the Wilderness to God by Elisabeth Elliot (Servant Publications)

The Desert Experience: Personal Reflections on Finding God's Presence and Promise in Hard Times by various contributors; Tommy Barnett, ed. (Thomas Nelson)

Appendix 4

Helpful Resources

Death of a Child

The Compassionate Friends
877-969-0010
www.compassionatefriends.org
The phone number will put parents in touch with someone who can direct them to a local chapter.

American SIDS Institute
2480 Windy Hill Rd., Ste. 380
Marietta, GA 30067
800-322-SIDS
www.sids.org

Mothers Against Drunk Drivers (MADD)
511 East John Carpenter Freeway, Ste. 700
Irving, TX 75062
800-GET-MADD (800-438-6233)
www.madd.org

Death of a Spouse

Parents Without Partners, Inc.
1650 South Dixie Highway, Ste. 510
Boca Raton, FL 33432
561-391-8557
www.parentwithoutpartners.org

Serious Illness

American Cancer Society (ACS)
1599 Clifton Rd.
Atlanta, GA 30329
800-ACS-2345 (800-227-2345)
www.cancer.org

National Hospice and Palliative Care Organization
1700 Diagonal Road, Ste. 625
Alexandria, VA 22314
800-658-8898
www.nhpco.org

The American Parkinson's Disease Association
1250 Hylan Blvd. Ste. 4-B
Stratton Island, NY 10305
800-223-2732
www.apdaparkinson.com

West Coast Info:
10850 Wilshire Blvd. Ste.730
Los Angeles, CA 90024
800-908-2732 or
310-474-5391

Spina Bifida Association of America
4590 MacArthur Blvd. NW, Ste. 250
Washington, DC 20007
800-621-3141 or 202-944-3285
www.sbaa.org

United Cerebral Palsy
1660 L. Street, NW Ste. 700
Washington, DC 20036
800-872-5827 or 202-776-0406
www.ucpa.org

Leukemia and Lymphoma Society
1311 Mamaroneck Ave.
White Plains, NY 10605
800-955-4572 or 914-949-5213
www.leukemia.org

Lupus Foundation of America, Inc.
1300 Piccard Drive, Ste. 200
Rockville, MD 20850
301-670-9292
www.lupus.org

National Alliance for the Mentally Ill (NAMI)
Colonial Place Three
2107 Wilson Blvd. Ste. 300
Arlington, VA 22201
800-950-NAMI (6264)
703-524-7600
www.nami.org

Murder/Abuse

National Organization for Victim Assistance (NOVA)
1757 Park Rd., NW
Washington, DC 20010
202-232-6682 (counseling line)
800-879-6682 (information and referral)

Victims of Violent Crimes
P.O. Box 3036
Sacramento, CA 95812
www.boc.ca.gov

Victims Assistance of America
www.victimsassistanceofamerica.org

Women Escaping a Violent Environment (WEAVE)
P.O. Box 161389
Sacramento, CA 95816
916-920-2952 (crisis line)
www.weaveinc.org

Suicide

1-800-SUICIDE (800-784-2433)

1-866-334-HELP

www.yellowribbon.org (teen prevention)

Acknowledgments

This workbook has been the culmination of fourteen years of working with those who were facing a loss or deep disappointment. The words, ideas, and lessons represented here could not have been possible without three special groups of people.

To the professionals in the area of helping people, let me say that I truly respect your work and your commitment to Christ and his people who are hurting. I want to specifically honor:

Rev. Chuck Swindoll, pastor of Stonebriar Community Church and founder of Insight for Living: for all of your writings and daily teachings that have influenced me to be a man of genuine humility, total transparency, and absolute honesty. Without your spiritual insights I would have strayed far from the path of righteousness.

Dr. Neil Anderson, founder of Freedom in Christ Ministries: for teaching me who I am in Christ and providing me with the tools to walk in my freedom in Christ. Your contributions to the lessons on forgiveness have personally blessed me and, I know, will touch those who journey through their grief.

Elisabeth Elliot, former missionary, and author and conference speaker: for sharing your pain in such a gentle way through your writings. You are a model of grace and of God's grace in our lives.

Dr. James Dobson, founder of Focus on the Family: for encouraging millions of people to hold on to their faith even when God doesn't make sense.

Dr. Billy Graham: for teaching me that in the midst of the storms of life, God is there, always inviting us into a relationship with him.

Dr. Timothy LaHaye: for your wonderful writings and insights in the area of anger.

Dr. H. Norman Wright, Christian counselor: for pioneering the way in the study of crisis counseling. I have learned so much from you that has helped me help others.

Sealy, Susan, Curtis, and Kate Yates, attorneys and friends: for not letting me quit. For believing in We Care when no one else did. For reminding me, sometimes daily, that it is never about us, and always about him.

Mr. Robert Dail, Chairman of the Board, We Care Ministries: for holding me accountable on every trip, and for being my companion and friend.

Rev. Jeff Jones, We Care Ministries: for your steadfast commitment to friendship.

Rev. Jeff Brawner, Senior Pastor, Bonita Valley Christian Center: for your sermons on anger and pain shared in your Four Tons of Canaries Series. I have never known anyone who is a finer orator, or one who works as hard as you do to prepare the meal for God's people on Sunday mornings.

Rev. David Schutt, Christ Community Church: for your Sunday morning messages which are always right on.

Dr. Grace Ketterman: for your words of guidance on managing anger.

Katie Maxwell, author and conference speaker: for your continued work with the bereaved and the initial challenge to think out of the box when we are serving them.

Doug Manning, former pastor and author: for your insightful works on grief and pain.

Dr. Alan D. Wolfelt: for remembering the children, and for your work in the area of children's grief.

Again, to each of you I say thank you for allowing me to build upon what you have taught in an effort to reach hurting people throughout America.

The second group are those whom I have been privileged to work with over the past fourteen years. I have traveled the pathway of grief with you, and you have shared your personal experiences with me so I could offer your stories here. Thank you for allowing me to come into your lives and families. You trusted me in your most vulnerable time.

To the Cassinelli, Perkins, Dail, and Bryant families, I say thank you for your strength to share your stories amidst the pain of your loss. To the Perez, Buckner, and Hilmann families, thank you for staying firm in your faith and modeling godly character through your loss. To the People of OKC and NYC, thank you for modeling steadfast love to the world as we shared your loss. To the people of Rockville, Maryland, thank you for your courage not to give into terrorism. To the students and faculty of Cleveland Elementary School and Olivehurst High School, thank you for reminding us that children also grieve.

The final group is, without a doubt, the group to whom I owe the most thanks. Without them, there is no We Care. There are no books. There would be no seminars or resources.

To my wife and ministry partner, Cathy: my love for you grows deeper as we continue to celebrate our victories, defeats, and adventures. You really are the author of this work, because without your encouragement, inspiration, and humor, none of this would have come to completion. I love you, Sweetie.

To my children, Kimi, Kyle, and Katie: thank you for allowing me—on your birthdays, graduations, back-to-school nights, and many holidays—to be shared with people who have needed a touch in the middle of the night. I am so proud of each of you.

To my mom and dad and ten brothers and sisters: thank you for loving me even when I don't call, for praying for me on a moment's notice, and for allowing me to share our stories with the world.

No list would be complete without a special thanks to the One who first loved me before I ever loved him: my Savior, Jesus Christ. To You I owe everything because without You I am nothing.

We Care Ministries

Services and Programs

Everyone experiences difficult moments as they are confronted with death. Often many decisions have to be made which require additional support during your time of need.

We Care Ministries is a non-denominational organization devoted to providing compassionate mercy to communities and individuals in times of crisis. Our mission is to provide care to families, individuals, and friends who have experienced a traumatic loss.

When disaster strikes a church, school, office, home, or nation, the We Care Crisis Response Team meets practical needs on the scene. The teams are trained to offer critical incident stress management and educational assistance throughout the event.

Over the past 12 years, We Care chaplains have ministered in times of crisis at national disasters including the Oklahoma City bombing, San Francisco earthquake, and 68 days at Ground Zero. In addition, they have provided care to teachers and students after schoolyard shootings and served the people of Maryland during the recent sniper attacks.

We Care has a host of resources, including the audio tapes for this Grief Workbook, to help you in your time of need. The twelve audio tape series is a supplement to this workbook which can be reviewed at the We Care website located at *www.wecare4u.org*. You will also find excellent resources to assist you with children's unique issues.

We Care team members minister to local congregations by sharing messages about overcoming adversity in times of crisis. Moreover, team members travel throughout the country teaching seminars to individuals and groups who want to learn how to work with people who are hurting in their local community. If you would like to book a seminar you may contact Susan Yates at (714) 835-3742.

If you have any questions, would like to discuss having us come, or would like the We Care team to help you or your community in any way, please feel free to call or e-mail us at anytime.

WeCare4u@softcom.net, www.wecare4u.org

A Step-by-Step Program for Small Groups or Individuals.

Grief is a natural, although at times overwhelming, emotional response to any type of loss. Whether your loss has been as a result of death, divorce, illness, or separation, you need to know that your grief is not something to be avoided, but a God-given process to be embraced.

The Grief Recovery Workbook is a step-by-step, self-guided journey through the grief recovery process. It is also an excellent resource for group study or for anyone who wants to be a compassionate-care provider.

Through his service in professional crisis care, "Chaplain Ray" Giunta and his wife have helped thousands of people work through issues of grief. In this workbook, he explores various aspects of the recovery process, including:

- **learning to live without the fear of future abandonment**
- **enjoying fond memories without painful feelings of loss, guilt, and remorse**
- **acknowledging and talking about your feelings**
- **forgiving others when they say or do things that are painful**
- **restoring your faith in God and your desire to care for loved ones**

As an added bonus, this workbook also includes a CD with personalized guidance for looking beyond your loss and reaching out to others, as well as prayers from Chaplain Ray himself.

CHAPLAIN RAY GIUNTA has been working in professional crisis care since 1987, after an early career in law enforcement. Cofounder and chaplain of We Care Ministries, a nonprofit organization providing intervention through compassion and training to individuals and communities in crisis times, Giunta has served at national disasters in San Francisco, Oklahoma City, and elsewhere, and spent sixty-eight days at "Ground Zero" following the 9/11 tragedy. He and his wife, **CATHY,** have taught "Healing the Brokenhearted" seminars nationwide. Chaplain Ray is also the author of *God @ Ground Zero.* www.wecare.org.

INTEGRITY
PUBLISHERS®

www.integritypublishers.com

ISBN 1-59145-024-1

90000

9 781591 450245

9 781591 450245

$19.99 US